Myths & Memories

Gilbert Adair is the author of *Hollywood's Vietnam*, which studied the American cinema's treatment of the Vietnam War, and *Alice Through the Needle's Eye*, an acclaimed Lewis Carroll pastiche. Much of his adult life has been spent in Paris, where he launched his career as a film critic and scripted *The Territory*, a 'philosophical exploitation movie' by the Chilean director Raul Ruiz.

Gilbert Adair

Myths &
Memories

FLAMINGO

Published by Fontana Paperbacks

First published in Great Britain
in 1986 by Fontana Paperbacks,
8 Grafton Street, London W1X 3LA

Set in Linotron Ehrhardt

Made and printed in Great Britain by
William Collins Sons & Co. Ltd, Glasgow

à la mémoire
de R.B. et de G.P.

Contents

Memories

Acknowledgements

'The *Nautilus* and the Nursery' was first published in *Sight and Sound*.

'Derrida Didn't Come' was first broadcast on the BBC radio programme *New Premises*.

The poems by Craig Raine from which lines are reprinted in 'E.T. and the Poets' are from his book *Rich*, published by Faber and Faber, and are quoted by kind permission.

Preface

This book is a centaur: which is to say, its nature is essentially *double* — as though, on the body of one creature, I had grafted the head of another. In fact, neither of its two sections can claim to enjoy a privileged position. They are, I trust, complementary texts, texts complementing each other as much in their differences (of approach, of subject-matter, even of linguistic style) as on those levels at which they interconnect (as Wittgenstein suggested, differences resemble each other more than similarities do). Before explaining why they have been published together, however, it might be useful to encapsulate what it is — individually — that they endeavour to achieve.

In the first section I examine, in essays of varying lengths, a number of contemporary British myths, mostly though not exclusively appropriated from the cornucopia of popular culture, and of a range extending from a TV quiz show to a tabloid headline, from Speakers Corner to the Booker Prize. Why, though, in describing an event as factual, as incontestable, as the Booker Prize, let's say, should I employ the word 'myth'? Basically, for two reasons.

One, though man as a social being has an aptitude for investing such a phenomenon with a single, reductive meaning (e.g. the Booker Prize is a substantial sum of money annually awarded to an English-language novelist for a particular product of his or her pen) and leaving it at that, it has, in reality, as a culturally determined operation, become encrusted with innumerable other meanings — meanings which are often paradoxical in their implications and have, in any case, little to do with the singleminded pursuit of literary excellence. These secondary meanings — or *connotations* — are what this section of the book is primarily concerned to explore. And to demonstrate how 'natural' it is for such connotations to acquire a mythic aura, let me consider an example which I have not treated in essay form: 'the *Guardian* reader'.

What is *de*noted by the phrase is straightforward to the point of tautology: anyone who buys and reads the *Guardian*. And, were one to undertake an analysis from that datum alone, one would probably be tempted to identify the *Guardian* reader as a purely statistical (or sociological) figure, definable by his adherence to a class or classes (mainly upper and lower middle, one presumes), a professional status (the liberal professions), a political party (SDP or non-Militant Labour), and so on. Yet, as we are all aware, 'the *Guardian* reader' has gradually come to emit another, *con*noted and more culturally coded message, one which the newspaper itself is prepared to endorse — parodically, at least — by publishing its weekly Posy Simmonds comic strip. This, the 'mythic' *Guardian* reader, in essence the classic 'woolly liberal', prominent in the demonology of the Right ('gay militants, lesbian mothers, *Guardian* readers'), might cursorily be defined, for the sake of simplicity, as the genuine article supplemented by what one would call an *ideology*. Though, naturally, such a pseudo-Platonic ideal has never existed, his identity, as an ideological concept, is more potent by far than that, necessarily unfocused and diffuse, of the reader as a pure statistic. He is 'consumed', to borrow from the terminology of Marx and Sartre, even by those to whom the category is derisively affixed. Thus, in a recent British film, *Loose Connections*, about a non-smoking, vegetarian feminist who advertises in a personal column for a like-minded co-driver with a view to motoring across Europe, the two eventual travelling companions identify themselves at their first meeting by copies of the *Guardian* under their arms rather than by the traditional carnations in their buttonholes. The newspaper is quite consciously made to function (not merely for the protagonists' benefit but for that of the film's audience) as a sign of their supposed compatibility, therefore of their respective sociocultural identities.*

The myths of which I am speaking, then, tend to be most plausibly expressed as *signs*, signs of the falsely evident, of what-goes-without-saying, of the victory of a (simple and seductive) stereotype over a (complex and daunting) reality.

Two, as many readers of the above will already have gathered, I also employ the word 'myth' as both a reference and a homage to the French writer Roland Barthes and, notably, to his most widely read and accessible work, *Mythologies* (originally published in 1957, it appeared in a somewhat abridged English-language version in 1972). Under that title, Barthes grouped fifty or so brief but densely argued reflections on some of the more tenacious myths informing the daily life and culture of his native country. What preoccupied him – and what he profoundly distrusted – was, on the part of those media whose task it is to define and diffuse that culture, the wilful confusion of Nature and History and the reassuring notion that every 'cultural' manifestation, be it a wrestling bout or a national dish, could therefore, secure in its single, inalterable meaning, be *taken for granted*. For Barthes, on the contrary, French culture was 'coded': that which seemed evident was falsely so; what he perceived around him was a perpetual bombardment of signs and signals and messages, all of them requiring to be

---

*Interestingly, the (male) applicant, a smoking, meat-eating football supporter, uses the *Guardian* to send out a deliberately misleading signal.

read, i.e. deciphered, for all of them might be masking some latent ideological abuse. He regarded himself, in consequence, as not only a semiologist (semiology is the science of signs and symbols) but as what he termed a 'semioclast' − beyond his frequently witty and startling insights lay the ambition, not exactly to demythify (for he never pretended to be the repository of any capitalized truth), but certainly to subvert, to *expose*, in the sense applied to (albeit with methods infinitely more subtle than) investigative journalists. Roland Barthes was a master of *idées refusées*, as one says *idées reçues*.

I am not Roland Barthes (though I have diverted myself, here and there, by pastiching his style); I am not even, by training or discipline, a semiologist and assuredly do not demand that my reader be one: my mythologies are anything but 'specialized'. Simply − like, no doubt, many another admirer of Barthes − I often found myself entertaining the delightful fantasy that the mass culture of my own country might one day be subjected to a similarly half-intuitive, half-'scientific' scrutiny. And since no such work existed, *eh bien*, I decided to write it.

Listed in the second section of the book are 400 (or, depending on the count, 399) 'memories' − slivers of memory, rather − a handful of which are strictly personal in origin, most of which are shared, and all of which begin in an absolutely identical manner: 'I remember' (except for an occasional, and insignificant, variation solely for reasons of rhythm). The shortest is three words long ('I remember' followed by the single-word object of the memory), the longest 155 words.

Of what, precisely, do these Dinky Toys of memory (I remember Dinky Toys . . .), these tiny shards of a common nostalgia, consist? They are, and I quote:

. . . little fragments of the everyday, things which, in such and such a year, everyone of more or less the same age has seen, or lived, or shared, and which have subsequently disappeared or been forgotten; they were not worthy of being memorized, they did not merit inclusion in History, or in the memoirs of statesmen, mountaineers and movie stars.

They might well re-emerge, nevertheless, several years later, intact and minuscule, by chance or because they have been sought out, one evening, among friends: it might be something that one had learned at school, the name of a sports champion, a crooner or an up-and-coming starlet, a song which had once been on everyone's lips, a hold-up or a catastrophe which had made headline news, a bestseller, a scandal, a slogan, a custom, an expression, an article of clothing or the way it had been worn, a gesture, or something even humbler, even more trifling, something completely banal, miraculously retrieved from its insignificance, fleetingly reclaimed, to produce, for no more than a few seconds, an impalpable little nostalgic *frisson*.

The preceding quotation, which might serve as an introduction to my own text, constitutes the 'declaration of intentions' of another French work by which I have been inspired, Georges Perec's *Je me souviens* (itself an offshoot of *I Remember*, by the American Joe Brainard, whose memories were, however, of a more privately autobiographical character). Unlike Barthes, Perec is still wholly — and scandalously — unknown in this country; but then, it has to be added in all fairness that it would take a brave and patient soul to translate, for instance, his magnificent *magnum opus*, *La Vie mode d'emploi*. As for *Je me souviens*, the fact of its being anchored in a French experience has rendered it definitively untranslatable; or rather, translatable only by way of the metamorphosis, the kind of total Anglicizing, which it undergoes here. For what, on my part, prompted the exercise was again that most elementary *Open Sesame* of wishful thinking: What if . . . ? What if, I would find myself dreamily fantasizing — what if such a book were to materialize in my own language, were to become part of my own culture?

Roland Barthes died in 1980, Georges Perec in 1982. Though it is difficult to imagine their not being familiar with each other's work, their names were never professionally conjoined during their own lifetimes; and it pleases me that, by my agency, two favourite authors of mine should now be united in posthumous, even spectral, collaboration.

But what is it that — from a reader's point of view — unifies the two sections of the book? This, perhaps: that the 'I remembers' were once also mythologies and the subjects of certain mythologies may in the future become the objects of someone else's 'I remembers'; that there is nothing more sheerly *democratic* than memory, unless it should be the readiness of a (not so new) theoretical discipline to reappraise the current codes and practices of mass culture; that it is incumbent upon a critic, a 'mythologist' — whose relation to the world, as Barthes himself confessed, is fated to remain 'of the order of sarcasm' — for once to acknowledge the potential charm (or, at the very least, the enduring *temptation*) of what elsewhere he is obliged to dissect; and, above all, that whereas in the first section I compulsively worry at, hound and harass my material, so that, exhausted, it might end by yielding up its fund of meanings and messages, in the second I am content to leave it blissfully in peace, to *let it be*.

Were one to see a horse with a man's head, one would not cry, 'Look! A horse with a man's head!' but 'Look! A centaur!' And were one to see a woman with a fish's tail, one would not cry, 'Look! A woman with a fish's tail!' but 'Look! A mermaid!' A centaur is a centaur, a mermaid is a mermaid. Mythological (in the word's more orthodox usage) as they are, such creatures have come to possess in our eyes (or in our imagination) their own compact and specific identities: if they are 'singular', then it is in the sense both of uniqueness and oneness. And that *double* singularity is what, ultimately, I might wish to claim for the book you are about to read.

Myths

A Mysterious Affair
of Style

If there is a single characteristic shared by each of the dominant critical methodologies of the last two decades — psychoanalytical, semiological, politico-ideological — it is what might be called an allure of improbability. *Now that is all very fine* — even the most intelligent and well-disposed reader, confronted with the cactussy taxonomy of any one of these angles of approach, is liable to say — *but what on earth has it got to do with my direct experience of the book in question?* The myth here is of an *apparatus criticus* existing in smooth, frictionless harmony with the very textures of the (literary or theatrical) text of which it is intended to act as the commentary (a myth, incidentally, which no one would think to apply to the more abstract, more rigorously unliterary discipline of music). On occasion it does happen, nevertheless, that this Common Reader, imaginary creature that he is, will catch himself artlessly expressing his appreciation of a book in terms more appropriate to the kind of analysis to which I have already referred; and this because, in spite of appearances to the contrary, he has been prompted to do so by its author. Such an author is Agatha Christie.

As we are often reminded, Agatha Christie is a novelist whose work is rivalled in sales only by the Bible and the Complete Works of Shakespeare (two volumes of such universally conceded prestige that they are allocated willy-nilly to the interviewees of *Desert Island Discs* as though indispensable aids to survival). Unlike them, however, her novels would never be considered the foundation stones of any new library; rather, they belong to a sub-species of literature commonly left behind in railway carriages or abandoned on the beach; as reading material, they are, so to speak, *tricks, one-night stands.* Yet it is they, paradoxically, which elicit from even the most unthinking of their consumers a genuinely critical response. So they cannot be regarded simply as illusionist works: the reader is alert throughout to the fact that he is dealing with a literary artefact, with something which had first to be written, to be produced.

A banal illustration, variants of which are to be found in virtually every Christie thriller, will suffice. A murder has been committed; the suspects have been assembled; and Hercule Poirot, chancing to be in the vicinity or else summoned there by a subsidiary character, begins his investigation. It transpires that a shadowy figure was glimpsed near the scene of the crime: a woman most likely, from the evidence of her clothing, but a woman — the witness adds in a pensive afterthought — of strangely mannish build. Forty pages or so later, we learn (casually, very casually) that one of the suspects had, as an undergraduate, taken part in some university revue, in which he had made a memorable impression as a female impersonator ... The innocent reader — by which I mean one unacquainted with Christie's narrative strategies — will as a rule respond to this second, seemingly corroborative piece of information by gleefully assuming that he has discovered the murderer's identity. His is an (elementary) form of deductive reasoning based, however, on an illusionist reading of the novel: i.e. the whole chain of circumstances may seem strained and highly improbable but, all in all, given these circumstances (which is to say, supposing them to exist outside the pages of a book), it is his solution that would most logically account for them.

The experienced reader of Christie knows better. Duly registering the suggestiveness of the evidence, he either withholds judgement or judges the clue too flagrant as a credible tip to that particular suspect's guilt or even, falling victim to the paranoia which detective stories wilfully induce, entertains it precisely because he suspects that its 'too flagrant' visibility may be a ruse to make him discard it. (There is no end, save in the asylum, to the pendulum swing of such an unresolvable dialectics.) In any event, and however frivolous the literary stake, he is certainly subjecting the novel to an anti-illusionist, therefore critical, reading. Not for an instant does he identify with its characters or their motivations; in a sense, he identifies with only one 'character' and her motivations: Agatha Christie herself.

Like certain modernist novels to which they otherwise bear no resemblance, Christie's thrillers are honeycombed with authorial insinuations designed to warn the reader that the book in his hand is a product of human artifice. Identical twins invariably give him pause, for instance, as does the proximity, at the scene of the crime, of a clock and a mirror (intimating that the dial may have been read in reverse); or any allusion to the 'black sheep' of a family shipped off in disgrace to Australia and supposed (but not quite known) to have died there. These are, of course, conventions peculiar to the classic English whodunit (a genre which Christie helped to pioneer with her earliest Poirot novel, *The Mysterious Affair at Styles*). The point is that the kind of reader to whom it would never occur to question the clichés of a Jackie Collins or an Alistair MacLean will *know* them to be conventions (even if the word itself does not form part of his vocabulary). And when he turns the last pages of a Christie novel (and here I ought to warn my own reader that I am about to reveal a few of her most famous twists), and discovers that the murderer of Roger Ackroyd is the story's first-person narrator or that the murder on the Orient Express was committed by, not one, but *all* the suspects together or that the perpetrator of the apparently agent-less murders of *Ten Little Indians* is none other than one of the 'victims', he treats each of these revelations less as some conclusive insight into a pathological mind than as *a feat of pure literary ingenuity*, to be judged according to the stimulation it affords him from that point of view.

Implausibilities, 'psychological' or other, cease to matter. What does matter is that, like two players hunched over a chessboard, reader and author lock themselves in combat, each openly acknowledging his adversary's existence and skill; and Christie's denouements may be compared to elegant endgames, if of a type set by Sunday newspapers, whose aphoristic concision has little to do with the true parameters of chess. (Chesterton wisely limited the narrative scope of his Father Brown stories to endgames alone, thereby sparing himself the ungrateful task of rendering their prehistory plausible.) The Christie reader is also, naturally, a detective, not identifying with Poirot but operating independently of him, sifting the clues which have been strewn in his path by an author whom one might consider a murderess by proxy (a designation encouraged by her rather ghoulish public image, of a bespectacled old dear with an incongruous partiality to homicide). But the most apposite analogy (albeit one from which Dame Agatha herself would no doubt have recoiled in horror) is sexual. Every admirer of her work will be familiar with the enervating sense of unfulfilment induced by one of her weak, or overly contrived, endings. Is it fanciful to propose that what the reader is seeking throughout the novel is his own ultimate release from its suspense: in short, an *orgasm*? Yet not only must he properly 'come', his orgasm has to be synchronized with that of the novel itself. For if he should 'come' first (if he should, with absolute assurance, deduce the murderer's identity before the final chapter), or if the novel should 'come' first (by the revelation of an unsatisfying murderer, motive or method), his frustration can be a truly terrible thing to behold. If all is well, though, his ecstasy will be tempered only, and *in extremis*, by what one is now obliged to call 'post-coital melancholy'.

Cleaning and Cleansing

The British make poor capitalists (or so we are informed); to begin with, they distrust, even despise, advertising. How else can one explain the diametrically opposed attitudes adopted towards it by those who scrawl graffiti in the London Underground and in the New York subway? In the Tube, advertising posters offer the graffiti artist a field of operation practically unlimited in its variety and invention, and he deprives himself of none of it: moustaches, punk mottoes, obscene appendages and florid feminist slogans dispute its walls for the commuter's attention. By contrast, in New York — whose subway trains in particular have been 'tattooed' with a brio and an energy to put our own rude practitioners to shame — not an inch of free space is spared *except that of advertisements*. There, even the most chronically dispossessed appear prepared to endorse the legitimacy of the 'haves'. In this country, again, the appeal of television commercials (by repute the best in the world) is often measured by the success with which their directors and copywriters have contrived to *disguise* the purely mercantile nature of the product — by which I mean, not the article being promoted but the commercial itself. Advertising is the art of the epiphany: the most effective ads have the compacted intensity, *toutes proportions gardées*, of a haiku. In a fair proportion of British TV commercials the product on offer becomes almost a McGuffin, as Hitchcock would say, a narrative factor of no great significance in itself except insofar as it generates a brief fragment of fiction, often droll (e.g. the Cinzano ads with Joan Collins and Leonard Rossiter), a video clip (most youth-oriented ads), a *Red Balloon*-type of 'poetic' short (I recall such an ad promoting Milton Keynes), etc. Yet there exists one kind of commercial which has stayed doggedly loyal to the more prehistoric conventions of the medium, and I intend to consider it here.

I refer to the advertising of detergents, soap powders, floor waxes and the like − screened in the afternoon and therefore for the attention of housewives. The mystificatory devices which these commercials deploy are always the same few. There is the interview-test (a supermarket customer is persuaded to betray her regular brand as a result of having unknowingly shown a preference for the superior effects obtained by that being advertised); the 'friendly hint', by which any less than pristine linen is insidiously invested with the social stigma reserved for body odour (two women compare with a remarkable absence of spite the relative whiteness of their laundry); and the magic, paradoxically irrational, invocation of science, usually in the form of a self-styled, quasi-alchemical 'formula' − *Cleansing Ingredient FX−4*, to coin a hypothetical but by no means caricatured example − mixing the indefinably progressive and futuristic (the letters composing such formulae are invariably those held at present to be rather arcane − Q, X, Z − but presumed likely, notably by writers of science-fiction, to gain widespread currency in some eternally postponed 'future') with the medicino-biblico-moral (detergents do more than clean, they *cleanse*). Since, in his essays 'Soap Powders and Detergents' and 'The Publicity of Depth', Barthes has already brilliantly demonstrated how some of these products encourage our apprehension of depth as a value ('Omo cleans in depth'), it might be worth concentrating for a moment on how others mythologize the antithetical but equally value-bearing state of *the surface*.

I have in front of me two floor detergents, one a Johnson product, the other from the Ajax line. Each of these vaunts its respective merits, whether of preparation or result, and on each the logo is preceded by the magic formula *New Formula* (for the word 'formula', in this context, is itself a formula). Each, moreover, has elected to illustrate its potency with the same minuscule fetish-image. An oblong segment of tiled kitchen floor, of chequerboard design, has just been traversed by a mop bearing the mysterious fluid. The two outlying areas of the floor as yet unmopped, uncleansed, and which previously might have looked clean enough, suddenly strike one as sad, grey and lacklustre by comparison with the dazzling swathe of immaculacy transecting them in the manner of a Nuremberg spotlight (the analogy with light being reinforced by the tiny scintillae which the floor literally gives off). Now, despite the smallness of the image (it works better on television, where the before-and-after process can be enacted in sequence), I experience what I can only describe as a certain euphoria at the sight of that chequered design 'overlaid' by another motif of light and shade, cleanliness and (relative) dirt. And when I ask myself why this should be so − for I don't give a fig for either Ajax or Johnson − I stumble across one of those simple truths of which everyone, perhaps, is aware but no one ever speaks about and of which one is all the same impressed to discover that advertising (and the least sophisticated, most basic type of advertising at that) has preserved the secret: which is that cleaning, in itself, procures for every human being an obscure sensual gratification.

Naturally, all of us have flinched from a sinkful of dirty dishes or a basketful of soiled laundry, as witness the popularity of dishwashers and washing machines. Yet, the more we depend upon such devices, the more we deny ourselves a deliciously instinctive pleasure, recoverable (though intermittently and by proxy) through advertising. It is the pleasure of making clean, of making smooth: e.g. the pleasure (which it is, let's not forget) of picking one's nose until the little cavernous enclave of each nostril presents a perfectly even surface to our probing finger; the puerile pleasure of decapitating a scab, 'planing' it away until it conforms to the unbroken, downy smoothness of the skin; the pleasure, finally, of scouring a grease-caked pan (this pleasure, indeed, reaches a sort of paroxysm when confronted with 'cakedness') until it gleams like new. In short, the pleasure – which, strangely, appears the height of natural-ness and also the height of artifice – of the *seamless*.

It is claimed that we sleep in order to dream, that it is from deprivation of the latter rather than of the former function that insomniacs suffer. Similarly, it may well be that, beyond the sociomoral dictates of personal and domestic hygiene, we clean – our bodies or our homes, compulsively or indolently – *in order* to gratify ourselves with the prospect of such emergent seamlessness. In which case, these advertisements are more 'sophisticated', more profoundly responsive to our psychic needs, than one has ever been disposed to believe.

The Philistine Factor

It would be an intriguing project to write a comparative history of philistinism, something which — to my knowledge, at least — has never been attempted. I mean, a chronological study of the various imprudent and unconsidered absurdities to have been pronounced on the subject of art since first the trinity of function, technique and expression coalesced to form the condition of the artist as we currently understand it — a turning point which, in the context of modern history, we can safely date from the Renaissance. And it is in the margin of that as yet unrealized project (which exceeds both the ambition of this book and the limitations of my own very relative command of art history) that I should like to examine two significant instances where what I call the 'philistine factor' has proved by no means negligible. The former has a bearing on the High Renaissance, the latter on the whole modernist tradition; the former is of interest because philistinism has exerted its influence (in the sense intended by Borges when he proposed that the status of a work of literature could be retroactively modified by those subsequent texts in which its influence is detectable) through a mythologizing process, the latter by demythologizing the object of its scrutiny.

The former is the Mona Lisa. It may sound impudently perverse to ascribe to philistinism the virtually universal admiration in which this painting is held, considering that Leonardo was without question a great artist and his portrait of 'La Gioconda' a masterpiece. Even so, if the Mona Lisa is now an all-purpose icon, as open to Surrealist defacement as to the parodic deformation to which she is mercilessly subjected by advertising (with the result that the original has become scarcely less 'invisible', scarcely less *ravaged*, than the same painter's 'Last Supper'), it is because of what millions of untutored observers — neither critics nor art historians — have consented to find in her. And what these observers esteem, surely, is what is odd, not good, about the painting. We pay a visit to the Mona Lisa — as to its rhyming homologue, the Leaning Tower of Pisa — as to an aberration, an eccentric, man-made aberration as there exist similar aberrations in nature: e.g. the Blue Grotto in Capri. The Mona Lisa smiles as queerly as the Tower of Pisa leans; her eyes, as everyone knows, follow one around the gallery — which is, when all is said and done, unnatural. But another word defines equally well her bizarre appeal: the word 'kitschy'. Though kitsch most commonly results from juxtaposing, with a superb indifference to the dictates not merely of utility but of artistic propriety, a number of inherently conflicting codes (as in the photographs of the Baron von Gloeden, in which the poses and props of a conventional, codified Antiquity are grafted on to the grubby, proletarian bodies of young Sicilian gigolos), the term can also be used to describe the ultimate, definitive uniqueness of any artefact so devised.

As with Tretchikoff's notorious 'Green Lady', for instance, in which the austere hieraticism of High Renaissance portraiture blithely coexists with the cheap exoticism of Chinese restaurant decor (and of which, in a way, the Mona Lisa might be considered the fine art equivalent), the popularity of Leonardo's painting is based on the sublime fashion in which it weds two not necessarily congenial aesthetic conventions: that — technical and painterly — of illusionistic modelling and that — anecdotal and perhaps,

13

where Leonardo himself was concerned, unwitting − of the 'enigma'. The 'enigmatic fallacy' is a classic condition of kitsch (the supposed 'greatness' of most paintings in Hollywood films is predicated on a *secret* which they are said to be harbouring*), in part because it draws the eye and mind 'beyond' the portrait into the mists of the psychologically ineffable (who or what was the Mona Lisa thinking of? Who or what caused that mysterious half-smile to play over her lips?), in part because it equates the artist's gifts with an imitative virtuosity of a type which art historians would more comfortably attribute to the oleaginous textures of a Bouguereau or an Alma-Tadema (i.e. if the ability to capture a resemblance is already the sign of a good painter, then the ability to convey a state of mind − indeed, the most ephemeral, most incommunicable state of mind − must be the sign of a great one).

That is, surely, what philistinism admires in the Mona Lisa; and, by correspondingly qualifying our own enthusiasm, the rest of us (whose approach to a work of art is determined by a consciously assumed culture and education) have obliquely endorsed its judgement. For who among us would ever confess to believing it, as its universal reputation would have us do, the world's greatest painting? Who would ever admit to a fondness for it untempered by irony?

Let me now take a contemporary, and more personal, example. I have sometimes felt a decided unease when confronted with the creations, respectively, of Henry Moore and Wassily Kandinsky, an unease patently occasioned by more than mere lack of affinity on my part. It is not simply that I remain unstimulated by the work of either, but that something at its core impresses me as irreducibly banal. And I have asked myself whether this conviction might not derive,

---

*It was, though, a European film which most brilliantly parodied the fallacy: Raul Ruiz's *L'Hypothèse du tableau volé*.

by whatever circuitous route, from the fact that — in (philistine) television skits, films and especially newspaper cartoons — a 'modern' sculpture is *always* represented by a slab of stone or wood with suavely curved, almost 'maternal' surfaces as well as, unfailingly, a hole in the middle:* in other words, a Henry Moore; and that a 'modern', i.e. abstract, painting (often 'set up' to be hung upside-down or squinted at quizzically) is *always* a random, free-floating mélange of geometric forms and those amoebic ideograms generically known as squiggles: in other words, a Kandinsky. Not an Epstein, Brancusi or David Smith, not a Léger, Klee or Mondrian (though on occasion, to be sure, a Picasso, in particular the kind of post-Cubist portrait 'whose ear is where its eye ought to be'), always a Moore and a Kandinsky.

Why so? Naturally, one is tempted to attribute such naive simplifications to the cartoonist's technique of caricatural distortion. Cartoonists, however, do not so much create as reflect a system of sociocultural mythologies: the reader's pleasure is due less to his acknowledgment of a witticism than to his delight at finding his own (obscurely articulated) prejudices so limpidly purified in the ellipsis of the artist's draughtsmanship. Thus he immediately accepts these diminutive Moores and Kandinskys as the symbols of modern art — and, of course, of 'what's wrong with it'. And if, on that (admittedly, highly dubious) foundation, one were to develop a critical approach towards the artists in question, if one were to investigate, solely on internal evidence, why they alone have come to represent the crudely derisive archetypes of contemporary sculpture and painting, one might find oneself drawing conclusions of this order: that Moore's work, *whatever its quality*, epitomizes the rhetorical grandiloquence that is the bane of too much modern sculpture, with the demiurgic artist 'rolling up his shirtsleeves' to turn himself

*A hole: paradoxically, the infallible emblem of modern sculpture.

15

into the humblest of artisans, breathing life and beauty into inchoate matter, grappling with his recalcitrant material like a boxer or wrestler until he has invested it with an 'interiority', a meaning — in short, the whole macho-ecological side of sculpture as an art; also that, in Kandinsky's 'hard-edged' period, *whatever its quality*, the cluster of geometric, pseudo-Zodiacal and perkily amorphous shapes often appear mechanical and overdetermined, leaping out at us and shrieking 'This is *abstract* art!'; that his paintings display an excess of abstraction as, in the finicky sumptuousness of Bouguereau or Alma-Tadema, there could be detected an excess of figuration (which is what we mean by academicism), as though, rather than 'being', they paradoxically 'represented', non-representational art.

It would be grotesque to claim that such intuitions exhausted criticism of either of these artists, or constituted anything more than one individual's (no doubt whimsical) response to their work. They do illustrate, nevertheless, the fact that, on a personal as well as a global level, what we dismiss as philistinism can boast a degree not only of influence but even, sometimes, of insight.

Seriously, Though

No one can fail to have observed, on television, on billboards and in newspaper advertising, the kind of charitable appeal (generally soliciting on behalf of some medical campaign: muscular dystrophy, cancer research, etc.) which, the better to communicate the gravity of its message, exploits the popularity of a TV performer. Perhaps the most curious feature of these appeals is their tendency to induct personalities from the realm of humour – Harry Secombe, Ken Dodd, Ernie Wise and, in a slightly different register, such light comedy actors as Paul Eddington and Richard Briers; and one is tempted to ask why.

In the mentality of the commissioning bodies, one may suppose the interpenetration of two widely entertained beliefs relating to comedy. First, is the clear implication that, while no human being could decently withhold sympathy from those afflicted by whichever malady is seeking financial assistance, a comedian is nevertheless required to traverse a far greater distance from his spontaneously 'natural' state of jollity, a distance which he will cover only if it should be justified by the cause in question: that, in short, nothing less than muscular dystrophy (particularly if suffered by infants) is calculated to wipe the grin off Harry Secombe's innately jovial features. Second, and ambivalently contingent upon the first, is the apparently indestructible theme of the clown as Pagliacci, obliged to laugh and make an audience laugh while convulsed, 'underneath', by inexpressible melancholia: thus who more suited to articulating an empathetic bond with his fellow-unfortunates? (There is also, no doubt, in Secombe's case, the discreet insinuation of a certain mythological Welshness, based on the dialectics of coalmining [an instantly legible symbol for 'the downtrodden'] and choir practice [the downtrodden's desire to raise their eyes from the mud towards the stars].)

Whatever one's scepticism vis-à-vis charity as a sufficient response to any problem, medical or not, these causes are without exception 'good'. Why, then, does one feel uneasy when confronted with such appeals, when confronted with Secombe wearing an emphatically sober suit and tie (the superlative pathos of the clown in mufti) as well as a countenance which it would be impossible to interpret as expressing anything but the deepest compassion (compassion being, precisely, the spiritual equivalent of charity) or with Ken Dodd, his jack-knife hair miraculously straightened, his trademark buck teeth all but imperceptible?

The problem is not merely one of representation — the fact, as we know, that these photographs were taken, not by some providential amateur who happened to come across his subjects in a conveniently pensive mood (actually *thinking* of muscular dystrophy or the need for cancer research) but by a professional, and in a professional studio, where they were requested, at a moment's notice, like the professionals they themselves are, to objectify unsuspected depths of sensitivity — but of overcompensation. The faces are *too* solemn, the compassion *too* unalloyed. And we may already have been witness to the telescoped process whereby such performers are accustomed to bridge the chasm between a programmed goofiness and a no less programmed assumption of all the world's truth, beauty and pain. For who has not seen Harry Secombe abruptly change styles when about to sing 'Men of Harlech' accompanied by a male voice colliery choir? Or Ken

Dodd, after a typically lascivious aside to the audience, smooth down that shock of hair and, announcing the transition with 'Seriously, though . . .', offer his arrangement of 'My Way'? One is, I'm afraid, reminded less of the twin masks of Comedy and Tragedy than of that old music-hall trick of transforming facial expressions behind a swiftly, vertically gliding hand.

It is not my intention to question the 'sincerity' of Secombe and Dodd (even a crocodile must occasionally shed real tears), only to indicate how that sincerity (invariably authenticated, in their appeals, by its ultimate signifier: a personal signature) may also become a commodity, an act, a mask; how, in the meantime, muscular dystrophy and cancer research may risk seeming as consequential as 'My Way' — as consequential, but not more consequential. Let them remember, too, not that comedy is itself a serious affair — an overly well-thumbed show business adage — but that, from Aristophanes to Brecht, it has been put to serious ends; and that, instead of exposing their personalities to a schizophrenic disjunction from which they must inevitably emerge the double losers, they would be better advised to discover a means by which it is through their humour that they address themselves to the real world.

Actors Acting

It is one of the crueller paradoxes of the theatre that, the wider the stage, the more difficult it is to retain one's balance on it, the brighter the lights, the less likely one is to be noticed. For anyone who inhabits it, the state must feel rather like a giant trapdoor; and one perfectly understands why an actor, even when momentarily relieved from the pressure of his role (i.e. when called upon neither to speak dialogue nor perform 'business'), should find it so awkward to relax, to cease pacing the stage like a caged panther grazing invisible bars. Even in repose, it would seem, his 'meter', unlike a taxi's, continues to run; though the audience's attention has been specifically focused on one of his fellow performers downstage, it ticks away, noisily and implacably, in the background. There may be a laudable vocational conscience behind such industry, except that an actor's job is not at all analogous to that of an office clerk, who, fearful of attracting the eye of his superior, takes pains to appear continuously busy, even overworked: it is of a qualitative, rather than measurably quantitative, order; and is, or should be, at the service of a dramatic ensemble, comprising the whole cast, the sets, the musical accompaniment, if any, and the play itself. In the best of cases, actors ought to be decoys, not cynosures.

I am speaking here of English actors: for it is, I believe, a vice particularly endemic to this country's classical acting tradition (a vice inherited from a handful of great pre-decessors — but not everyone can be an Olivier or Gielgud or

Richardson). Consider the Royal Shakespeare Company, and almost any recent production there of a play by the dramatist to whom its name pays homage. What one's ear immediately registers is that, for an actor like Alan Howard (a notable offender), not even something as basic as *respiration* has been permitted to escape his histrionic vigilance. He inhales and exhales *actorishly*, with every breath he takes – and much clipped teeth-sucking between phrases – emitting a meaning and a message. It is rather as though the author of some more or less subtle, more or less ambiguous, text actually felt the need to have printed 'between the lines' (in a different typeface, perhaps) what he intended us to read there. As for the question of delivery, the inspiration is, as I suggested, an actor such as Olivier, who – notwithstanding his immense talent – always gave the impression of *playing himself playing a part*. And it is to Olivier's film of *Richard III* (a record of his stage production) that one can no doubt trace the robotically brittle declamation of Shakespearean verse which has become practically the RSC's house-style. Thus, when Olivier delivers the play's opening monologue, he stresses its prosodic components in a manner that seems arbitrary and totally unselective:

Now. Is the. Winter. Of. Our discontent.
Made glo. Rious summer. By this. Sun of York, etc.

The effect is akin to that of the little white cartoon ball which, in Hollywood musicals of the thirties, would rebound from one word to the next of some popular song to enable the cinema audience to accompany the performer on screen; or, more precisely, of library books defaced by the pencil underscorings of a previous borrower: arduously as one strives to ignore or defy these alien, intrusive emphases, one nevertheless finds oneself pondering, against one's will, just

21

why this or that passage has been so favoured. So it is with a certain species of actor: by subordinating poetry, meaning and nuance to the intimidatory stress pattern of an over-determined scansion, and by substituting his own respiratory prowess for that of the dramatist's verse, he imposes a single, coercive reading on the spectator, who, dispensed from the need to understand the text (the actor obligingly performs that service for him), is left with the sole commission of admiring its interpreter. That is a genuine source of pleasure, to be sure, but also a limited one.

A similar process of mystification can be seen at work in the British cinema, though the question there is of faces, not voices. (The difference between theatre and cinema actors is that, while the former must project, the latter are projected.) As an art form, and contrary to the theatre, the cinema responds more to the contours of a face, and to its *grain*, than to any expression it might assume (e.g. Garbo's face as an exquisite Rorschach Test in the climactic shot of *Queen Christina*): it constitutes a museum of faces, a Prado of faces. Rare, unfortunately, in our own national cinema, is this concept of the physiognomy as a *tabula rasa*.* A British actor's face tends to be as corroded by his experience − or simply by his vocation as an actor − as an alcoholic's by gin. That of a Trevor Howard, for instance, a Denholm Elliott or a Michael Palin comes, as it were, preceded by its expression (of, respectively, disillusioned rectitude, dishevelled caddishness and ingratiating earnestness). Their professional personae have definitively *set* − the way one was warned, as a child, that a grimace would adhere to one's features were the direction of the wind to change. As a result, they − but also innumerable others − are faced with just two

---

*An unforgettable recent exception, however: Miranda Richardson as Ruth Ellis in *Dance with a Stranger*, with her chrome-gloss hair, her tawdry *volupté* and her masklike, floury white, unbreakably porcelain face − a face like a breast on which someone has pencilled a face.

equally cramping options: to be typecast; or, which amounts to the same thing (since it is the actor's typology that remains foremost in the spectator's mind), to be cast 'audaciously' against type.

Like his theatrical counterpart, the British film actor has not been trained to relax, to let go; to achieve the affecting stillness, the glorious laziness, of a Gary Cooper or a Robert Mitchum — no, even within a single frame enlargement, he can still be seen madly acting away. Yet this, too, is a discipline, an indispensable discipline most of our actors, alas, have yet to acquire: how, and when, *not* to act.

Listomania

Like one of those magazine covers which depict a typical reader in the process of reading a smaller version of the magazine which one is oneself in the process of reading and on whose cover is seen an identical reader reading a still more miniaturized reproduction of the same magazine on whose cover . . . and so forth — potentially, at least — *ad infinitum*,* the *Guinness Book of Records* can be found magically inscribed within its own pages. In effect, under the rubric 'Best Sellers', we learn that the 'world's best selling copyright book is the *Guinness Book of Records*' and that its sales are 'now nearing 50 million copies and increasing by some 50,000 per week'. There is, in this remarkable record, what might be termed a luxury of connotation. Not only does the book's self-inclusion within its own 'vision of the world' (and if any work of literature can claim a vision of the world, it is the *GBOR*) legitimize the accompanying entries — entries which might otherwise have risked being dismissed as of minor, frivolous or even dubious value — by reassuring the reader that his own enthusiasm has been preceded and vindicated by that of millions of his fellow human beings, it also reinforces the *almost* supernatural aura with which the book manages to enhalo the accumulated objects of its attention.

And it is precisely in that 'almost' that can be located the publication's charm. The *GBOR* reconciles the supernatural (a vague yearning for which, it is reasonable to assume, is

*There is a French expression for such a figure: *mise en abyme*.

24

instinctive to every human being) with the real; so that the *fantastique* — for so long the frustratingly exclusive preserve of fiction (and, for most of us, accessible outside of fiction only by way of the hand-me-down testimony of some friend of a friend who may once have encountered a ghost) — becomes, no matter how improbably, that of fact (which confers upon it a supplementary prestige). In a work of fiction (a fairy-tale, let's say, or a Latin American novel of the school of 'magic realism') the presence of a character nine feet tall would impress us as an invention, a literary conceit; met with in the *GBOR* — i.e. the pre-acromegalic giant Robert Wadlow, whose height was 8'11" when he died at the age of twenty-two — the abnormality inspires a very different kind of *frisson*, it being a property of the supernatural that it is most effective when sanctioned by the natural. (That said, it should also be pointed out that the 'supernatural' annotated by the *GBOR* responds to a single metamorphic criterion: not that, rich in fictional possibilities, of the anagrammatic — the *fantastique* as an anagram, as an ingenious rearrangement of the natural order — but of the purely numerative. Thus a man who kisses a woman, however passionately, cannot aspire to inclusion, whereas Jonathan Hook, who kissed 4106 women in an eight-hour span, is assured of a place in its Pantheon.)

There exists another book which, on an incomparably more elevated plane, also sought to naturalize the supernatural (a book, moreover, cited in the *GBOR* as being 'the world's most widely distributed'): the Bible. If emancipated from the exaltation of spirituality, the Bible can equally be read as a chronicle (more often 'exhaustive' than truly narrative) of the world and its wonders; and its idiom, no less than that of the *GBOR*, has frequent recourse to the superlative mode: the Most High, Most Exalted, etc. There is even a Biblical 'style' — a sort of incantatory itemizing of facts and figures, whose most easily detectable (and parodiable) sign might be that chiming fetish-

25

word of the Authorized Version, the verb 'beget'. And it is not impossible that what lends a millennial, slightly apocalyptic tone to the *GBOR* and, indeed, to the whole contemporary mania for 'list books', for taking inventories − be it of the world itself − is nothing else but the faint echo of those Biblical rhythms. (Nor need one look so far: a mere dictionary, too, is a form of Bible, one in which words beget words, and which abounds in parables, proverbs and 'morals'.) Furthermore, just as the Bible does, the *GBOR* invokes a number of barely credible catastrophes (a Chinese earthquake in 1556 in which an estimated 830,000 people perished) and marvels (a geyser in New Zealand which erupted in 1904 to a height in excess of 1500 ft), it has its floods (1.50 inches of rainfall recorded in a single minute in Guadeloupe in 1970) and its fires (a lava flow of 4.35 miles in Iceland in 1783), its saints (Professor Frederick Sanger, the only Briton to have been twice awarded the Nobel Prize in any category − not to mention the numerous record-breaking pole squatters, onion peelers and golf ball balancers who are beatified every year) and its martyrs (Roy Sullivan, an American Park Ranger who has been struck by lightning no fewer than seven times).

Perhaps, then, the unparalleled sales of the *Guinness Book of Records* can be attributed to the way in which it satisfies one of our enduring needs: the need to believe in *miracles* (whether almost or wholly supernatural is of minor import), to believe that the planet which we inhabit is still on occasion capable of being brushed by the sacred. And if somehow 'spiritualized' (for what it crucially lacks is a theology), and appropriated by some half-demented guru, it might yet become the Holy Scripture of an age in which mankind has renounced its traditional God but not the desire to extend its spiritual frontiers. Cults, after all, have been founded on less.

Jargons

I spoke, in my preface, of the science of signs, semiology (or, to employ a more familiar and near-synonymous term, structuralism). I did not, perhaps, sufficiently convey the importance which, in the last two decades, it has assumed in France, Italy, Germany and the United States: for the more advanced thinkers of these countries, the 'fact' (social, political, economic, literary or whatever) has henceforth acquired a vital new property: its sign, its signifying identity.

And, meanwhile, in this country? What, for the vast majority of *our* literary critics, is structuralism? A 'fashionable' methodology, of course — 'fashionable' in this context implying ephemeral, inherently impermanent, already de-vitalized by the germ of its imminent obsolescence. It is as though the English language were eternal and immutable, the shared heritage of a shared culture, which an 'alien' discipline such as structuralism — but the same applied to Existentialism and Marxism and psychoanalysis — can only *contaminate*. Structuralism, moreover, communicates itself not through the medium of a language, but through that, infinitely less noble, of a jargon;* and the basic unit of this, as of any, jargon is a (fresh-minted) cliché. Those homespun clichés from which even ideally unsullied usage cannot be

---

* *Jargon*, in the OED: 'Applied contemptuously to any mode of speech abounding in unfamiliar terms, or peculiar to a particular set of persons, as the language of scholars or philosophers, the terminology of a science or art, or the cant of a class, sect, trade or profession.' And: 'Often a term of contempt for something the speaker does not understand.'

exempt ('variety is the spice of life', 'avoid like the plague', etc.) are mildly, almost affectionately, censured as the marginal, regrettable but, alas, inescapable by-products of language as a repository of human (i.e. universal) verities; those which have been imported with the 'fashionable' linguistic sciences (and, to be sure, they do exist) suffer instant excommunication (or ex-*communication*).

Such observations, I suppose, are themselves now the clichés of the progressive Left, and next to no purpose would be served by deciphering a code which was cracked long ago. Yet one has become so used to reading snide denunciations of any intellectual system whose articulation requires that one do more than merely draw upon a currently available kitty of abstractions that it might be worth taking a hard look at this Platonic ideal of language which, for its custodians, is being infiltrated by neologistic inelegancies. It does appear, in effect, to be an endangered species (purity in language, as elsewhere, is not within everyone's means) but a near-pristine example (virtually a museum piece) can be found in the journalism of Bernard Levin and, more particularly, in a collection of his essays published under the robustly Georgian title of *Enthusiasms*. As it happens, Levin has unflaggingly castigated, notably in his weekly column for *The Times*, what he perceives to be the neo-philistinism of theoretical (or, in his lexicon, 'pseudo-intellectual') jargon; and reviewing a polemical work on clichés, he described English in its current usage as 'being reduced to a stock of television catch-phrases eked out by the vile language used today by politicians, trades union leaders, social workers, civil servants and churchmen' (it would be interesting to examine the prominence accorded to social workers in the demonology of the Right). Very well; but what do we find in *Enthusiasms*, an effusive 'defence of pleasure' and languid promenade through those satisfactions in which its author indulges with especial gusto: books, music, *haute cuisine*, cities (no risk here of his being credited as fashionably cerebral and modern)?

A jargon, if a bewhiskered one. Levin's soul itches and, on page after page, he cannot resist scratching it in public. Seeing himself as tragically at odds with the contemporary world, like a piece of china in a bullring, he takes refuge in eternal values (but what a fatal sense of routine that word 'eternal' betrays!), discoursing on music as though it were food, on food as though it were music, and omitting in the process to enlighten the reader on either. No matter what may have been Levin's original intentions, the book offers not much more than the complacent spectacle of his own quivering sensibility.

Thus, the rather wonderful disregard for banal socio-economic conditions (a man of modest means 'cannot eat at the Gavroche, but he can eat at the Gay Hussar' — Levin's notion of modesty seems to begin where a social worker's ends); the calculated manipulation of political realities (to reinforce his thesis that 'most people are happy most of the time', Levin instances the statistic that 'since the bombing and killing began in Northern Ireland, the incidence of nervous and mental disease in the province has gone *down*'); the dour, overtly self-gratifying mandarinism ('I fully expect to be, and quite soon now, the last living man who knows the difference between a colon and a semi-colon'); the wholly *curricular* tastes, obviating the slightest need for adventurism or even choice (Austen, Dickens, Shakespeare, Homer, Cervantes, Melville; Mozart, naturally, whose 'depths cannot be fully sounded by any human being', and Schubert ['No meal I have ever eaten could be truly compared to a performance of Schubert's *Death and the Maiden* quartet by the Amadeus on their finest form . . .'], Beethoven, Wagner and Bruckner; Van Eyck ['Arnolfini's Wedding' is 'an amazing thing'], Giorgione ['La Tempesta': 'that strange and inexplicable thing'], Rembrandt ['paying my respects once more to "The Night Watch", and winking back at Rembrandt's laughing eye'] and Vermeer); the collection of dreary French quotations, not one of which will be unfamiliar to a professional after-dinner humanist (*l'appetit vient en mangeant, le mieux est l'ennemi du bien, si jeunesse savait . . .*); and finally – when confronted with the ineffable, whether natural or man-made – the moist excretions of affectivity, in which the sole argument put forward for the magnificence of a painting, a landscape or a *soufflé au saumon* is that, paradoxically, of the observer's *inarticulacy*, his ecstatic, swooning abdication from the merest hint of a critical response ('There was no river too turbulent, no mountain range too high, no desert too arid, for men to wonder what lay on the other side . . .' 'Anyone capable of appreciating through music the wonders and the mysteries of the human soul cannot fail to emerge from *Fidelio* in a state of spiritual exaltation . . .' and so on, and on).

It is easy – not to say, child's play – to mock Levin's faith in 'fine writing', his threadbare neo-Georgian discursiveness, his 'farting through trumpets' style. The point worth making, however, is that it is not only he but the very language in which he writes – a language satisfying every imperative of 'organic' autonomy and every condition of self-contained and self-perpetuating 'purity' – that is bereft of ideas. Whatever meanings it may once have been capable of generating, there is absolutely nothing remaining to be said in an idiom which can refer without irony to 'the wonders and the mysteries of the human soul' or to works of art as pointing the way 'to our human understanding of our human duty, the duty to be transformed, to rise from darkness into light, to pursue the will-o'-the-wisp of integration and completeness until it turns out to be no will-o'-the-wisp but the shining sea of eternal truth'. Heraclitus said (in an aphorism obsessively quoted by Borges): *no one bathes twice in the same river;* Levin's rhetoric is as stagnant from overuse as boarding-house bathwater. For what is the use of vilifying jargon in an idiom which is itself an exhausted, retrograde jargon? What is the use of avoiding linguistic clichés if everything one says, everything one thinks, *is* a cliché?

On First Looking into Chaplins Humour

Charlie Chaplin remains, in his posterity, what he never ceased to be during his lifetime: a maverick, a dissident, a mischief-maker. Persecuted for almost six decades by the self-appointed arbiters of moral, political and ideological orthodoxies, he now finds himself posthumously assailed in the one category in which one had always supposed him to be impregnable: the aesthetic. For his detractors, apparently, Chaplin usurped the rank once universally accorded him as the century's supreme clown. Not only are his films politically naive, flawed by an excess of pathos and not all that funny (*sic*), he himself was a boorish, mean-minded man, ungenerous 'to a fault' and consumed by jealousy of his co-performers: the refrain, for anyone conversant with current film criticism, has become a wearily predictable one. There even exists a suitable candidate for the pedestal from which Chaplin will be ejected when the dismantling of his reputation is complete: Buster Keaton. The problem is not just one of critical disharmony: it actually appears as though Keaton's advocates chafe at the notion that one should admire Chaplin at all, let alone the more. Each to his own taste, naturally, and one might well leave it at that. Yet Chaplin's achievement seems to me a living model for our impoverished contemporary cinema; so that I would like to propose, not a theory (I am far too partial and subjective for a theorist's severities), but, at least, an accessible back door or tradesman's entrance into his deceptively transparent oeuvre.

Keaton, to start with, was an aristocrat. He detached himself from the world like one of those ethereally distracted figures in illuminated manuscripts whose enhaloed, apostrophizing forefingertips overreach the confines of the frames encasing them. Even when that skittish yet indomitable goose-step of his would irresistibly accelerate into a sprint by, it seemed, the winding of some giant, invisible key, he seldom abandoned an air of slightly spooky other-worldliness. Chaplin's physical agility was of a different order: it brought to mind a dapper, accomplished roller-skater who could not quite get the hang of turning corners without skidding. Though he was regularly the butt of style-conscious critics for what they perceived as his insensitivity to visual effects, he could whip up a bravura sequence if so inclined (the lighter-than-air *mappemonde* of *The Great Dictator*) and he devised gags every bit as amazing as Keaton's. In terms of their resonance, frequently more amazing: I am thinking, for instance, of the transatlantic steerage crossing in *The Immigrant* where he rolls dice while the ship rolls him. *The Immigrant*, in fact, one of his earliest masterpieces, is as good a point of departure as any for my modest thesis. Chaplin, it should be recalled, himself had entered the United States as an immigrant Englishman; and, in his autobiography, he would savour the poverty he had suffered as an infant with an almost parodically Dickensian relish. On the other hand, he was soon to become the cinema's single most prominent luminary, and as such was assuredly familiar with Soviet propaganda classics and the warped and jagged creations of German Expressionism. What he absorbed from the latter movement, however, was not the signifier — weird perspectives, evilly brewing shadows and all — but the signified, the thing filmed: the ghetto. Chaplin was, and stayed, the film-maker of the ghetto experience; of, in a word, *dirt*.

'Dirt', as a suffusive visual odour, so to speak — the scurfy piggishness of Stroheim, of Buñuel in his Mexican period, of the French directors Clouzot and Duvivier on occasion – is a filmic configuration for which the cinema would seem to have lost the formula. The 'sordid' it knows how to film (*Raging Bull, La Lune dans le caniveau*), if by that we understand either flamboyant putrefaction or a raffish, idealized, strobe-lit squalor, 'laundered' (in the word's literal as well as its Mafioso connotation) and homogenized. But, in Chaplin's films, certainly up to *Limelight*, the sets are (or impress one as) grimy, the very light is filtered through the clinging, festering haze of the slums – in a sense unintended by his critics, they *stink*. And Charlie himself? Naturally, he stinks. How could the paradigmatic 'little man' not do? Crudely phrased, one's apprehension of gamey underclothes is often quite overwhelming; and a reader tempted to dismiss such a contention as altogether uncouth and trivial might be reminded that, technically, underclothes constitute an immanent kind of off-screen space and may therefore be regarded as a minor aesthetic parameter (as was indeed the case with Stroheim's fabled and finicky vestimentary perfectionism).

Even as a millionaire and the idol of millions, Chaplin never dodged this implication of his persona (unlike Jerry Lewis, who, as an ungifted, down-at-heel circus clown in *Hardly Working*, sported a glaringly conspicuous Cartier wristwatch throughout the film as though to assure fans that he, Jerry Lewis, the incredibly rich, thriving and adulated comic, was playing a character role). And the 'vulgarity' of his humour never betrayed the etymological root of the word, 'of the people' (unlike Mel Brooks', which is merely a shortcut to laughter, just as slow motion tends to be a shortcut to beauty). It was from this *total* identification with the *lumpenproletariat*, with the material and physical realities of its quotidian existence, that Chaplin's admittedly sometimes off-putting sainthood derives. Keaton was a great artist, to be sure, and his niche in the history of the cinema is an elevated one; but Chaplin belongs to history itself.

Britain Is a Democracy

In his essay 'Operation Margarine', Barthes wrote: 'To instill into the Established Order the complacent portrayal of its drawbacks has nowadays become a paradoxical but incontrovertible means of exalting it.' And furthermore: 'It is a kind of homeopathy: one cures doubts about the Church or the Army by the very ills of the Church and the Army. One inoculates the public with a contingent evil to prevent or cure an essential one. To rebel against the inhumanity of the Established Order and its values, according to this way of thinking, is an illness which is common, natural, forgivable; one must not collide with it head on, but rather exorcise it like a possession: the patient is made to give a representation of his illness, he is made familiar with the very appearance of his revolt, and this revolt disappears all the more surely since, once at a distance and the object of a gaze, the Established Order is no longer anything but a Manichaean compound and therefore inevitable, one which wins on both counts, and is consequently beneficial.' (*Mythologies*)

A fine illustration of such a 'vaccine' at work in Britain is Speakers Corner. Institutionally, every Sunday morning, a crowd of both native Londoners and bemused vistors assemble at the Marble Arch end of Hyde Park to listen to the on occasion eloquent and often violently worded theses of a half-dozen soapbox orators. Themes may vary from religion to politics, attitudes from the antimonarchist to the anti-clerical (the most titillating of the speeches are inevitably those which are *anti*), obsessions from the occult to the ecological; no less institutional than the speakers themselves, moreover, are their hecklers — though, in what is a slightly sinister development, the latter have tended to become increasingly concerted. Even if one may be allowed to marvel at the notion that a group of people voicing their opinions in a park should be regarded as an awe-inspiring phenomenon, one which makes this country the envy of the world, the spectacle (for that is how it is perceived) is frequently quite diverting, the more so if one attends it without the illusion of being enlightened or converted; and it is probable that Londoners contemplate the whole amiable institution with the same superstitious fondness which they accord to the ravens in the Tower.

In truth, notwithstanding the ideological polyphony, the sheer Babel of voices confronting the casual spectator, all of those participating, speakers and hecklers alike, are actually, unwittingly, saying the same thing: *Britain is a democracy*. By sanctioning such a localized representation of revolt, as Barthes suggested, the State is seen to have established its credentials as a defender of free speech; for, by a paradox familiar, and dear, to the governments of Western democracies, nothing more surely attests to freedom of speech as a political reality than the fact of an individual publicly (freely) alleging that it has been muzzled. Yet it might well be remembered that being authorized to make such a claim *here* does not eliminate the eventuality of its being more 'literally' tested *there*. Should you, in Hyde Park, proclaim that the Thatcher government is the most chronically authoritarian, dishonest and regressive in non-communist Europe, you are likely to be treated to the indulgent smiles of a couple of police constables stationed on duty; put forward an identical argument in the streets of Brixton and Toxteth or on a miners' picket line and the official reaction, qualitatively and quantitatively, is liable to be of a very different order.

No one would take fundamental issue with the unified 'consensus' of Speakers Corner: Britain *is* a democracy. But, with a country which, more frequently than any other, has been brought before the European Court for having violated certain basic human rights, which vindictively avenges every infringement of the Official Secrets Act (even if, or perhaps especially when, the 'leak' has been demonstrably in the public interest), which is contriving to secure a virtual monopoly in the flow of information, the danger is that such institutions as the BBC (with its appointees vetted by MI5) and the national press (ever-increasingly the private property of a handful of staunchly reactionary 'barons') could find themselves transformed into equivalently peripheral and innocuous showcases of political independence. Freedom of speech on a soapbox is, of course, a perfectly authentic freedom for all that, one denied, as its apologists would readily remind us, to the ordinary citizens of both right- and left-wing totalitarian states. But freedom of speech on a soapbox may also come to resemble nothing so much as a statue on its plinth; and statues, as the ultimate stage of *rigor mortis*, tend to be erected to the dead.

Big Babies

Let's begin by considering a cruel hypothesis (cruel, for once, to be *un*kind): someone − anyone − I myself, let's suppose, why not? − arrives at early middle age gravely debilitated by an extreme, even pathological, form of infantile regression: which is to say, I am a chronic bedwetter, I burst into squally tears at the merest provocation, and so on. Normally, or so one might imagine, instead of jauntily assuming this unfortunate condition, I would seek out medical or psychiatric counsel; or else, if incapable of forgoing the psychic gratification which they induced, I would submit to the necessity of repressing such practices or only very clandestinely indulging them. In either eventuality, however − and this is the nub of the problem − there would be scant likelihood of my ever wholly adjusting to the condition, of my ever attaining peace of mind. In that case, perhaps, and if I were clever enough (or clever-clever enough, 'clever-clever' being, not twice, but half of 'clever'), I could have recourse to a third and more radical manoeuvre: I could turn my handicap into a *style*.

Here I use the word 'style' rigorously in what one might call (at the risk of the adjectival qualifier itself going out of style before too long) its 'Yorkian' sense − from Peter York, author of *The Sloane Ranger Handbook* (with Ann Barr), *Style Wars* and *Modern Times*, and the Petronius, the indefatigable arbiter, of *pis*-elegance. But before more closely examining the slippery implications of York's concept (and there is a certain ironic aptness in the fact that, now that literary criticism is seeing fit to expel 'style' altogether from its lexicon, the word should be travestied by a voguish middlebrow journalist – precisely as those fads, artefacts and watering-holes chronicled by York are 'dropped' whenever they start filtering down to the general public), it might be instructive to conjure up a mental image of just such a Yorkian guide to the hormonal disorder hypothesized in my opening paragraph.

The Big Baby Handbook (as it is presumably to be titled) would therefore contain a chapter devoted to Big Baby eating habits: sugar-speckled porridge consumed from a bowl with bunny rabbits along its rim and 'That's a Good Boy' inscribed in the middle; 'children's sweets' (i.e. Dolly Mixtures, liquorice sticks in sherbet); and, of course, lots of milk. Clothing: a bib for all meal-times; man-sized cotton nappies to be worn under pin-striped City suits and, in the utmost intimacy, regularly, deliciously, soiled; and daintily stitched rompers (purchased not, as was the case with the Small Sloane, at Harvey Nichols, Knightsbridge, SW1 [235 5000] or Please Mum, 69 New Bond Street, W1 [493 5880], but at some Soho emporium specializing in unorthodox sexual paraphernalia). Reading matter: such oft-thumbed classics (for, as they say, 'children of all ages from eight to eighty') as A. A. Milne, Beatrix Potter, Enid Blyton and, manifestly the Big Baby Bible, *Peter Pan*, etc., etc.

Where such an exercise in social rehabilitation is concerned, the function of 'style' is essentially *cosmetic*: it *coats*, rather than embraces, the condition of which it is the public expression; it constitutes the chic, prettified camouflage of a state of being which, were it to be exposed in all its clinical rawness, would risk revolting the non-affiliate. Its kinship is with one of those graceful feints deployed by a conjuror to distract the spectator's attention from the single significant stratagem by which his trick is effected; and if style here is still, to all intents and purposes, that 'envelope of substance' that it has traditionally represented for literary humanists, the envelope is closed, sealed tight. The reader (of York's work) is diverted from any real comprehension of a social reality and its ideological underlay by a seductive kind of mystification familiar from the essays of Tom Wolfe: the half-satirical, half-fascinated portrait of a 'life-style' accompanied — and, in a sense, defined — by the complacent inventory-taking of its (behavioural, vestimentary, residential) accoutrements.

With *The Sloane Ranger Handbook* the act of concealment is not too serious (and the condition is certainly not clinical). Beyond the verbal window-display of Huskies, Hermès headscarves and eligible (but, if possible, not over-pricey) public schools may be detected a stereotype of brainless, snobbishly selective consumerism such as has always existed and no doubt always will exist in the plummier Home Counties. Not, to be sure, a very attractive stereotype but, in the end, innocuous. (It should be said, moreover, that the book's huge commercial success probably derived less from the indulgently beady eye which it cast over the whole Sloane mythology than from the fact that it served as a consumerist catalogue for the attention of aspiring Rangers. That York and Barr knowingly fostered this ambivalence is confirmed by the pertinence with which they were able to spot the mechanism in a quite different context: in the section on Sloane literary tastes, they included Richard Adams' *Watership Down* with the rider that Sloanes were 'not interested in the allegory but it *is* set in Berkshire'.) The affair becomes more problematic when one turns to a subsequently published work — and virtual simulacrum of York and Barr's — *The Young Fogey Handbook*, edited by Suzanne Lowry.

The Young Fogeys — whose most prominent triumvirate comprises the novelist and critic A. N. Wilson, the architecture critic Gavin Stamp and Charles Moore, editor of the

Spectator — form a group of (more or less) well-known public figures, inducted from the worlds of journalism and academe, who pride themselves on being, as Lowry phrases it, 'old in everything but years', on having acquired 'the stoop, gravitas and quirkiness of an octogenarian don or a querulous country parson'. The confirmed Young Fogey 'dons dead men's tweeds and rides his bike to celebrate a lost world of Pooh and Pugin, an England as some great Edwardian nursery, secure, warm, smelling of toast and strong soap, full of richly illustrated storybooks, hand-carved toys and the best possible train set'. (As one may observe — Pugin apart — the Young Fogey's Utopia is located not a thousand miles away from that of my hypothetical Big Baby.)

Superficially, at least, one is free to find his petulant archaism attractively cranky or not: but is there any cause why one ought to be disturbed by it? I believe so and for two reasons.

One, unlike the Sloane Ranger, the Young Fogey enjoys easy access to the various communications media; and if Britain is at present a nation whose literature remains, on the whole, little translated, whose 'thinkers' are almost comically uninfluential, whose architecture is an international laughing-stock — a nation, in short, *whose intellectual life interests no one but itself* — it is in no small measure due to the cosy parochialism of which the YF represents the point of highest visibility. Two, it is, as with the Sloane Ranger, necessary to scrape away the coating of 'style' and reveal the ideological discourse which it strives to render palatable. Beyond the Bath Olivers and lopsided Fair Isle cardigans, what can one detect? Snobbery, of course, 'the great and incurable English vice'. (But why great? Why incurable? And, indeed, why English? Snobbery is above all a phenomenon of class.) Its companion-vice, rampant philistinism: according to Lowry, the Young Fogey despises abstract art, modern music, jazz and 'psychology' — by which term she evidently means 'psychoanalysis' (psychology is less a science than a universal human attribute from which even Fogeys, Young and Old, would be hard-pressed to escape). Sexism: the YF recoils from 'non-closet homosexuals' and once 'admired James Morris but finds his translation into Jan absurd and unnerving'. Racism: he owns to an acute suspicion of the Race Relations Act, albeit relishing the opportunity of parading 'recent social acquisitions or curiosities such as upper-class black intellectuals'. Elitism, expressed in a detestation of comprehensive schools, sociologists ('they confuse them with social workers,' says Lowry of YFs) and the vernacular — expressed equally in Lowry's quaint description (she is something of a Fogeyette herself) of Jeffrey Bernard's 'Low Life' articles in the *Spectator* as 'an indelible portrait of life in a 1980s gutter' (how many of those living in 1980s gutters are likely to recognize their plight in Bernard's column, one wonders). Finally, xenophobia: the YF, we are baldly told, 'stays away from Abroad'.*

Young Fogeys, Lowry further informs us, number Chesterton among their Top Ten Heroes. Perhaps, then, one might remind her of the question posed by Father Brown: 'Where to hide a tree but in a forest?' Where to hide a word but in a text? Well, the word here — whether she likes it or not — would seem to be 'fascist'.

---

* Notwithstanding the care taken by Lowry and her collaborators to avoid appearing the dupes of their subject-matter, the ideology disclosed by the above quotes *is* a latent one: *The Young Fogey Handbook* reads as a celebration rather than an exposé; and much, one feels, has been forgiven a religion of which the Old Testament God is Dr Johnson, the New Testament Redeemer Evelyn Waugh, the Holy City Oxford, and the host (in the liturgical sense) Fuller's Walnut Cake.

What Is Boy George For?

Somewhere the comedienne Hermione Gingold relates her dismay, when starring in an 'intimate' revue, at overhearing a little girl in the front row of the stalls ask her mother, 'Mummy, what is that lady *for*?' The question is by no means a stupid one. Here we find a child, confronted with a theatrical idiom ('sophisticated', slightly risqué comedy, one would imagine), which she is not old enough to appreciate. For her, therefore, the only intelligible aspect of the performance is a nexus of artificially heightened signs (make-up, footlights, applause) which, even to one of that age, connote a certain idea of *fame*. And it sets one thinking what a very strange thing fame is when it has been detached, as here, from the talent which originally generated it; when it is viewed as either an abstract sensitization, an aura, of personal prestige or else as a benign rumour preceding, then prompting, one's desire for what might lie behind it. The paradox is that, for the artist, fame is generally the fruit of an extended period of gestation, of *work*, whereas for the consumer the order is often reversed: it is by the artist's public persona that he is alerted to the existence of a body of work which he may then choose to investigate further; but if, for whatever reason, he chooses not to, what he is left with is fame in its pure, crystallized state, fame disconnected from any ostensible 'cause'.

With no knowledge of contemporary pop music, is it my turn to ask: What is Boy George for? To his fans (and he may well be very talented) the question must seem meaningless, or its answer self-evident. Yet not only is it one of the properties of fame that its influence extends far beyond an immediate circle of initiates, it is precisely at that stage that it becomes worthy of study. For the object of fame, however shallow its foundation, or ephemeral its duration, is always *functional*: in fact, no one ever became, according to the current formula, 'famous for being famous'; fame always annexes a previously vacant space, no matter that, a month before, one was unaware that the space was vacant or even that it existed at all. Though I have never consciously listened to one of Boy George's records, his notoriety alone signifies something to me: I ask myself what it might be. The first message I receive is, of course, vestimentary. So far as his clothes are concerned, the sign under which he appears to have been born is that of excess or extremism: half Geisha, half Peruvian peasant woman, he impresses me at once (rather more than most pop singers, however outrageous) as someone *on exhibition*. But a message of a different if related type is being sent out simultaneously: he is also, I am led to believe, a *sexual* extremist, an androgynous figure, identifiable by the customary extravagance of his clothes with transvestitism, and therefore (that false 'therefore' of Public Opinion, of what Barthes called the Doxa) with homosexuality. Even the sobriquet by which he is known helps to confirm such an impression: 'Boy' (an epithet which, strangely, assimilates the fact of his own [and every pop singer's?] eventual obsolescence:* will he be named Boy George at fifty?) carries a faint suggestion of the twenties, of bobbed hair, of flat-

*Such obsolescence, in Boy George's case, seems to have overtaken the publication of this book (bearing in mind, though, that it is sometimes imprudent to write *the obituary of Lazarus*, so to speak). His star, as I add this footnote, is already on the wane – his public 'image' has, at the very least, been considerably modified – and it should scarcely need to be specified that the subject of my essay is the Boy George of the first, androgynous phase.

45

chested *garçonnes*; 'George', an eminently masculine name, one borne by several English kings, has nevertheless been 'tainted' by equivocal, confusedly transsexual connotations: George Sand, George Eliot, *The Killing of Sister George*.

Yet the peculiar fascination of Boy George resides less in these messages themselves than in the way they have been obscured – scrambled, as it were – by the very extremism of his appearance, which is much too 'personal' for the codified stylization of the transvestite. The same is true of his make-up: though, again, it appears to reinforce the code of effeminacy, and 'therefore' of homosexuality, his is so thickly applied, so masklike, as to be more evocative of classic Japanese theatre – one might say that it 'transcends' sexuality.

Thus does he cunningly displace the ambiguity that would seem to be his stock-in-trade. With someone who is so theatrically costumed, coiffed and made-up, someone whose sexuality strikes one as so overdetermined, what one begins to doubt is not whether he is 'straight' but whether, indeed, *he really is homosexual*. And from that point a process of reinstatement may confidently be set in motion. (The strategy is similar to that of the bald man who wears a wig of thinning hair in the hope that his friends, observing that he *is going* bald, will forget that he *is* bald.) I do not intend to imply that Boy George is privately embarrassed by his sexuality, only that his public image represents a reversal of what one has always taken to be the natural evolution (of an individual, an ideology, a religious movement) *towards* an extremist position. Instead of ending up an extremist (as might be claimed for John Lennon), *he started out as one*, and then slowly, insidiously, proceeded to backtrack. Which means now that every acknowledgement of personal banality (or oddity) becomes permissible, since the subject (Boy George) approaches that banality from a diametrically opposed direction to our own, so presenting it to us in a new and unexpected light.

Thus, Boy George on sex: 'I'd prefer a nice cuppa tea' and 'I have been celibate for a year now'; on wealth: 'I still argue about the price of clothes in shops and I'm always trying to get a discount'; also his attitude to fame and how little it has changed him (as reported by a *Sunday Mirror* journalist): 'Recently I spotted him cycling around West London on an old beaten-up bicycle. I have even seen him sitting in a local laundrette, waiting for his washing.' Even when apparently owning up to sexual deviance, Boy George exploits the cunning escape-clause of bisexuality: 'I sleep with both girls and boys, but I'm neither proud nor ashamed of it. It's just a fact of life.' It may well be a fact of life, but it is above all a fact of society: bisexuality tends to be perceived less as the sexual Utopia towards which all of us would gravitate, were we possessed of healthier psyches, than as homosexuality 'up to a point' (in Evelyn Waugh's celebrated euphemism). Here, as in every other respect, what Boy George truly represents is moderation, not excess. Underneath his glittering crust, which is nothing else but the outward sign of his material success (like a Rolls, a yacht, a country house), squats a homely little lad, 'just like you and me'. So it ought not to surprise us that, besides his innumerable fans, he is reportedly cherished by their mothers and grandmothers (or, in tabloidese, 'mums' and 'grannies'). For this, finally, is what Boy George is for: to personify, in an age of the media, and of 'mediacrity', an age in which fame is institutionalized, piped into the home like Muzak — to personify, as I say, a curious kind of Everyman.

Fish and Chips

Heavy with significance as with cooking oil, handled as a culinary mythology with the delicate cutlery of quotation marks but eaten, so tradition dictates, with the fingers, fish and chips are not to be consumed lightly. Here is the first paradox of this apparently artless dish: so that it may enable every Briton symbolically — if only for a brief while — to reassert his national identity, his oneness with a culture in decline, its ingredients (staple foods in most parts of the world) must compromise theirs. For the *genius* of fish and chips derives less from their preparation (frying in deep fat is the zero degree of a cook's expertise) than from their combination. Thus they do not belong to the same culinary ideology as fish alone, whose reputed bloodless insipidity makes it fit only for pious Catholics (even then, however, limited to a single day a week: the obligation is clearly perceived as an act of self-denial) and effete gastronomes who, in any case, alter its taste and consistency by covering it with 'rich sauces' (as distinct from honest, proletarian sauce from out of a bottle). What chips bring to fish is not blood but the next best thing: their own pulpy and cohesive substance, which we have come to accept as the natural complement of blood, or rather meat, e.g. steak and chips. By this analogical association with the manliness of red meat, fish is invested with the qualities it appears most to lack: simplicity, virility, universality.* But it, too, works its counterinfluence: the

* There exist, of course, few foods more literally universal than fish; but the universality claimed by the fish-and-chips eater is one that levels out at his own socioanthropological category, not 'beneath' him (Third World fishing communities, etc.).

48

fact that, as served up, it is similar in presentation to the chips which accompany it (a brown crust on the outside enfolding a white mash inside) allows it easily to blend with them, forming a composite paste that enters the mouth without surprise and without friction, almost as though predigested, as though the palate were its proper habitat, the passage a mere formality. (The discovery of a fish-bone while eating fish and chips, for instance, comes as a mild shock.) The flavour is pungent and direct, so much so that the consumer is relieved of the necessity of *drawing it out*, of cultivating it; he does not experience any gustatory resistance. (It helps, paradoxically, that the British sprinkle both fish and chips with vinegar, which is a practice not encountered elsewhere, I think. Here, it erodes what differences remain in texture and taste between the two ingredients and, with its aroma, further weakens the resistance which I mention above.)

Oddly, even the phonetic consistency of the phrase has been affected. In the United States, where the word 'chip' means what we would call a potato crisp, it has retained the hard edge, the *bite*, of its original sense of a broken fragment of wood or metal. 'Potato chip' (or 'chocolate chip cookie'): enunciated, it makes as brittle a sound as a snap of the fingers. In British English, however, the same word, onomatopoeically mimicking its own signified, contrives to sound soft, moist, squashy — as though it, too, had sponged up vinegar; the effect is even more patent in 'fish and chips', with the 'sh' of 'fish' softening up the normally tougher 'ch' of 'chips'.

What does it mean to eat fish and chips? As, perhaps, *the* culinary sign of Britishness, it has been nationalized as much as socialized, with the result that it now tends to suspend rather than expose fundamental sociocultural distinctions. For those who eat it frequently, it is, as a meal, tasty, nourishing and cheap; also authentic, not a bastardized form of

49

something better (like a fatty cut of meat): rich or poor, whoever eats fish and chips eats basically the same dish. But for those who eat it more rarely, and for whom it can be considered a populist equivalent of quiche, it represents a simple, expeditious means of reconciling oneself with the world, no less: with one's family first of all (children adore fish and chips); then, with the 'ordinariness' which one fears even as one exalts it; finally, with one's 'roots'. Though the sphere of influence of any such dish is as modest as it is intermittent, fish and chips therefore constitute what one might call, whimsically, a force for national unity.

The *Nautilus* and the Nursery

Utopias have traditionally been predicated on the double principle of enclosure and repetition: enclosure in the sense of a 'wrapping around' illustrated by Barthes in his essay on Jules Verne — which is to say, the projection of a finite, private and uncontaminated enclave as an ideal of (bourgeois) comfort and sensuousness ('The *Nautilus*, in this regard, is the most desirable of all caves: the enjoyment of being enclosed reaches its paroxysm when, from the bosom of this unbroken inwardness, it is possible to watch, through a large window-pane, the outside vagueness of the waters, and thus define, in a single act, the inside by means of its opposite'); repetition in that the strength of this enclosure (a necessary guarantee of its privacy) must periodically be affirmed by submission to a series of tests (akin to algebraic variables), either superimposed or externally imposed upon it. Thus, through all the adventures which make up the narrative of *20,000 Leagues Under the Sea*, the *Nautilus* remains snug, larval and inviolate. There exist, of course, innumerable Utopias which are neither material nor literary constructs: these, being more diffuse, more latent, more 'ideological', are usually only accessible to an operation of decipherment. The classic Hollywood cinema of the thirties and forties, for instance, was essentially Utopian in design; its sense of enclosure was reinforced by such parameters of the studio system as typecasting, the regular recycling of plots and the remarkable constancy of character psychology; and serials or series of films (Tarzan, Sherlock Holmes – currently, the *Star Wars* saga) helped, by repetition, to throw this stereotypology of the world into even greater relief. Moreover, such recent films as *Jaws* I, II and III and the *Rocky* cycle have so reduced the pool of variables at their disposal that each succeeding episode has become practically, shamelessly, a remake or duplicate of the original model. (As may be seen, an 'advantage' of Utopian cinema is the facility with which it contrives to reconcile opposites: plots which are different but also the same, characters who age but do not, the work coming to an end yet theoretically capable of endless rebirths.)

The best-known instance of this phenomenon in the British cinema is no doubt the *Carry On* . . . series (now complete, it seems, though specialized trade papers regularly announce the ambition of its producers to film one last episode). *Carry On* . . . is Utopian cinema *par excellence*. Which is not, in itself, saying much; the question ought rather to be, which Utopia? For, as I have said, the *Nautilus*'s 'enclosure' is as material as it is abstract, it is even what is called 'well-appointed': a good, richly stocked library, a first-class cuisine, deep leather sofas and armchairs, and firm, heavy drapes. This reproduction of a nineteenth-century ideal of bourgeois luxury is clear enough, and what has been added is a layer of cultivated refinement that suggests nothing so much as the study of a man-of-letters. One might go so far as to say, Jules Verne's own study; certainly, such as Verne describes them, Captain Nemo's quarters aboard his submarine conform to the (then as now) popular, mythic conception of a successful author's abode (a myth perhaps less idealized but no less widespread than that of the candlelit garret in which the Bohemian *poète maudit* scribbled and starved). By projecting his own invulnerably plush environment on to the high seas, and into the future, Verne synthesized those otherwise unresolvable opposites of 'staying at home' (security) and 'travelling abroad' (adventure); *20,000 Leagues Under the Sea*, being no more than a writer's unashamed reverie, legitimizes the reader's most ingenuous daydreams; and, consequently, unlike the treacherous allegories of Wells and Orwell, it and Verne's other premonitory novels do not disturb: rather, they reassure, they tranquillize, they 'tuck the reader in'.

On those occasions when I have happened to watch a *Carry On* film (either professionally, as a critic; or more idly, precisely as a diversion from the exercise of criticism), I have experienced a similar sense of assurance, of social and, indeed, existential harmony, of 'things in their place'. Though the extrinsic settings may vary with each film (barracks, hospital ward, grammar-school classroom; or else the Khyber Pass at the turn of the century, the 'Merrie England' of Henry VIII), the 'world' proposed to us by the series in its entirety remains a vacuum as finite and compact as the *Nautilus*, since it is founded, not on measurable boundaries, but on an unchanging interconnection of relationships between the company of performers and the stereotypes which, from film to film, from epoch to epoch, they never cease to embody.

When all these settings, these modalities of time and place, are superimposed one on top of the other, as buccaneers were said to combine individually meaningless segments of a treasure chart, what ought to emerge, once the incidentals have cunningly cancelled each other out and only essential instructions remain legible, is the very blueprint of a Utopia; and the answer to that question 'Which Utopia?' — an answer I now offer like a television chef demonstrating the preparation of a complicated dish before pulling a perfect specimen from the studio oven — is, the ultimate address (one might almost say, the terminus) of all rational nostalgia: I mean, the *nursery*.

Whatever the overt 'intellectual' discourse of the series (a none too elevated one, to be sure), its true mentality is that of the playroom. Thus the films are also *escapist* – here, however, the word carries no exotic connotations, being used in the sense of 'regressive': they ease the spectator's regression into a warm, uterine pen, one in which human relationships and their crises have been emancipated from any real consequence or responsibility. Each of them (*Carry On Sergeant, Nurse, Teacher, Doctor* and so forth) represents a game, a giggly, off-colour charade, a tiny microcosm of the adult world, a *model world* (as one says 'model aeroplane'); and it is worth noting that the professions aped and parodied, especially in the earliest of the films (soldier, nurse, doctor, teacher), are traditionally the most favoured guises of those children's games which involve dressing-up. The actors, too, do not *play* soldiers or teachers – they *play at* them. In *Carry On Nurse* (perhaps the most popular, certainly the most prototypically 'rude' of the series: a 'bedpanorama of hospital life', etc.) what they are playing at, like generations of children before them, is Doctors and Nurses. And from the fact that, in such a context, giving a performance implies little more than donning a costume, or uniform, and in no way requires the actor to modify his 'act' in accordance with his character's supposed professional, social or intellectual status (Sidney James, for instance, whom one might regard as the 'Groucho' of the series, remains the same genial, lecherous Cockney whether he is impersonating a cab-driver, a town councillor, an eighteenth-century highwayman or Henry VIII), we may presume that audiences are alert to, and obscurely approve of, this primitive alienation effect.

In the same way, it does not matter that *Carry On Cowboy* was all too visibly shot somewhere in the Home Counties, since it is the very falseness of the landscape which clinches, as it were, the travestied nature of the whole enterprise. The producers had only to crown the green and gently undulating English countryside with a sheriff's office, a saloon bar and a livery stable, like a schoolboy wearing a Stetson hat, and the trick was done. The game being played, it hardly needs to be added, is Cowboys and Indians (for some reason, no doubt because of its association with just such children's games, the word 'cowboy' has seldom figured in the title of any Western with pretensions to seriousness); and one can see — better, probably, in this film than any of the others — with what ease the more or less permanent repertory troupe invites comparison with a gang of children (or, at least, the comic-strip caricature of such a gang: Lord Snooty and his pals). There is the type of scheming ringleader mentioned already (Sidney James); the spindly but 'game' weakling (Charles Hawtrey); the snivelling, eternally complaining sneak (Kenneth Connor); and the upper-class prig (Kenneth Williams, in whose persona the codified signs of the [flamboyant] homosexual — effeminate gestures, a mincing walk, a falsetto voice — stop short of any definitive *implication* of homosexuality as a practice or an ethics, thereby enabling him to assume the ambiguous but immature and, in any event, infinitely less threatening identity of a 'sissy'). The feminine roles may be inserted without strain into the same stereotyped ideology: the fat, bossy spoilsport who can nevertheless be relied upon to nurture a secret passion for one of her playmates (Hattie Jacques); the neither-too-pretty-nor-too-plain girl who, in spite of her gender, is suffered fairly gladly by her male betters (Joan Sims); and the knowing nursery flirt, richly endowed with the one infallible sign of knowingness: a precocious physical development (Barbara Windsor).

And there we are, finally, at the question of sex. For what the *Carry On* . . . series is most notorious for is being 'naughty' — a word, yet again, also applicable to children and their misdeeds. But are its two meanings so dissimilar? To an amazing degree, the sexual practices and fantasies which recur throughout the series are those first ingested in the nursery: scatology; voyeurism (the term in English for a voyeur, 'Peeping Tom', even sounds like the protagonist of a nursery rhyme, notably 'Tom, Tom, the piper's [or peeper's?] son'); and the fad for genital self-measurement ('What a fuss to be making over such a *little* thing!' one of the nurses in *Carry On Nurse* teases poor Kenneth Connor, terrified as he is at the thought of having to strip in front of her). More subtly, there is a disturbing sense of grown men and women actually in the process of discovering, with a mixture of embarrassment and delight, the existence of physiological differences between the sexes. (Not unexpectedly, the common denominator of these four traits turns out to be the bedpan, a Grail-like receptacle for the *Carry On* . . . scenarists, whose almost too obvious analogy is with the 'potty'.) Thus the eroticism of the series has jammed at the fundamentally infantile stage of *disclosure*, in which nudity is a (never quite attained) culmination, rather than a point of departure.

Beyond citing Donald McGill's seaside postards and the British music-hall tradition, the critical Establishment has usually dismissed these films as unworthy of its attention. On the other hand, their commercial success has been considerable; and there is surely food for reflection in the fact of this − if not eternal, then oft-repeated − return, on the part of a substantial number of our compatriots, to the most formative and 'most desirable of all caves'.

'Barmy Bernie Moves In With Blonde'

'Barmy Bernie Moves In With Blonde': so read a headline published in October 1985 by one of Britain's tabloid newspapers (the *Star*, as it happens). The 'story' which it captioned centred on Bernie Grant, the black leader of London's (Labour) Harringay Council and a man who achieved a brief notoriety by publicly voicing the opinion, in the wake of a Tottenham riot during which a lone constable was brutally hacked to death, that the police had received 'a good hiding'. By the time the headline appeared, however (a week or so following the riot), the newspaper had become more or less indifferent to the immediate consequences of Grant's statement. The burning issue which it owed to its readers to blazon across the front page was the fact that, just after speaking out as he did — but, one presumes, for reasons entirely unconnected with his politics — Grant had separated from his wife and family to take up residence in the home of a (blonde) woman friend.

It is to be feared that the British tabloid press is by now a lost cause, and that next to no purpose would be served by further indicting its ineradicable crassness, mendacity and ignorance, the prurient vicar/choirboy syndrome and the rampant bingomania in all its up- and downmarket multiformity. The Glasgow Media Group, Henry Porter (in his book *Lies, Damned Lies*) and numerous other commentators have already covered the ground so comprehensively as to render additional exposition redundant. But the *Star*'s

57

headline (whose grotesque vulgarity reflects its conformity to, rather than any eccentric deviance from, current journalistic practice) alerts us to certain features of contemporary tabloidese which have not, to my knowledge, been subjected to investigation in any detail.

'Barmy Bernie Moves In With Blonde': what can one read in (or *into*) such a caption? First of all, on a prosodic level, the crude alliterative proximity of 'Barmy', 'Bernie' and 'Blonde' – an alliteration which functions, as in advertising slogans, less as a stylistic than as a strictly mnemonic device. It is intended to 'catch the eye' (and ear), to 'stick in the mind'. Yet this is already a trivial form of mystification: for, whether it be in a poem by Swinburne or a headline from the *Star*, alliteration always contrives to suggest that there exists a natural harmony between the two truths of sound and meaning, the sheer *manifestness* of the former legitimizing what might have seemed questionable in the latter. Since the reader is somewhere obscurely aware that, by calling into question the credibility of the phrase, he also risks compromising its alliterative pattern of sounds, the pattern which attracted his attention in the first place, he will complacently tend to accept them both in terms of equality and rightness. Thus, though it was nudged into existence by a quite fortuitous phonetic correspondence, the conjugation of 'Barmy' and 'Bernie' appears to him as almost 'hereditary'; and, with any luck, the epithet will permanently attach itself to the name like a Homeric metaphor.

As for the word 'Blonde', its lubricious sexual (i.e. sexist) connotations remain surprisingly potent and viable. In the popular mentality, apparently, blondes are still loose, licentious women of easier than average virtue and ampler than average bust measurements; and, by leaving his wife for a blonde, rather than for a brunette or redhead, Bernie Grant decisively undermined his (and, by extension, his party's) fitness to run one of London's borough councils. (Nor ought one quite to rule out the possibility of a discreet racist undertone here, given that Grant himself is black: which is to say, the precise racial antithesis of shiny 'Aryan' blondness.) Since, in fact, by any half-respectable standard, the story does not constitute news at all (and was consequently ignored by every serious national newspaper, of whatever political persuasion), its disclosure on the *Star*'s front page can have no imaginable purpose beyond that of bringing into disrepute both Grant *and* his views on the tactics deployed by the Metropolitan Police in boroughs with a heavily concentrated (and unemployed) non-white population.* To be sure, Grant's assertion was offensive and foolish − it displayed, to say the least, a gross tactical insensitivity − and he may well have been unfit to execute his duties as a councillor, but such an exhalation of verbal heat (in the shape of a barely disguised smear campaign) is no substitute for a real point of view, however simplistically articulated.

'Barmy Bernie Moves In With Blonde': the language used, then, is one of intimidation, not elucidation (a double intimidation − of both Grant and the reader). Which is news from nowhere, except that what has been remarked less frequently is the pernicious manner in which the intimidation extends even to the pseudo-vernacular idiom in which it has been couched. Curiously, the sole concession which the headline makes to traditional journalese is the omission of an indirect article before 'Blonde'. Otherwise, it is obviously aping what it supposes might be the vocal reaction of a 'typical' reader to such a revelation − or, to caricature (in *Private Eye*-style): 'Crikey, d'you see where that there barmy Bernie's moved in with a blonde!' Thus the *Star* not only

---

* One could argue that it was the item's sensationalist aspect which the newspaper sought to exploit − its 'spiciness'. Yet, if divorced from a specifically polemical framework, that seems far too meagre and tame to justify the front page.

tells its readers what to think, it tells them how they should express their thought.

Similar examples abound. One might reasonably have imagined it to be the reader's function, on hearing that the *General Belgrano* had been sunk, to bellow (if so inclined), 'Gotcha!': not at all, the *Sun* judiciously relieved him of even that pitiful obligation; or, 'What a bloody cheek!' at the notion that a child welfare officer might have resented dismissal after failing to act on the unmistakable evidence of an infant's maltreatment: no, the *Mirror* beat him to it; or else, 'Good on yer, pooftah!' at the 'amazing' announcement of Elton John's wedding: no, he was again scooped by the *Sun*. It is as though it were felt insufficient for these newspapers (now scarcely more than printed graffiti) simply to report the news (some of the news), they also judge it politic to pre-empt the reader's (doltish, stage-Cockney) outrage at that news – a reader who is, in any case, no less crudely stereotyped than the events and personalities set up for his preprogrammed indignation. This is no doubt what the British tabloid press likes to think of as its 'liveliness'.

Since, as we know, the combined circulations of the *Sun, Star* and *Mirror* (and there seems little reason not to add the *Mail*) far surpass those of the 'qualities', their contributors, editors and proprietors might well resort to the argument that they are merely 'giving the public what it wants'. Which is a dismaying thought. Yet if a typical, satisfied reader's response to such a headline is assumed to be something on the order of 'It took the very words out of my mouth', he should pause for a moment to reflect that the distinction between 'taking the words out of someone's mouth' and 'putting them in' is a fine one, indeed; and that such systematized ventriloquism eventually runs the risk of any occult relationship between master and puppet (as illustrated in a celebrated episode of the forties horror film *Dead of Night*): the dummy is maybe the ventriloquist's dummy, but the ventriloquist often becomes the dummy's dummy.

Still-life of a Life-style

Photography and Autobiography: these are (with the Theatre and the History of Art) two cardinal points of David Hockney's sensibility (his sensibility as a painter, not as the photographer he has become in recent years). Photography, first of all, remains a curious medium: considerably more venerable than the cinema, it has yet to establish, even in the eyes of some of its most prestigious practitioners, its own generic identity as an art; it tends to be defined, not by its essence, but by its *difference* (its difference from film, from painting). Though such differences patently exist, the most fundamental are perhaps, and deceptively, not those which spring to mind. One is tempted to claim, for instance, that film differs from photography solely by the articulation of movement. True enough, except if one includes home movies, which strike me as sharing, rather, the ideology of the photograph. Gone is the smooth narrative suavity of the (fiction) film: what I remark of movement in a home movie (indeed, as a bored and captive spectator, it is all I truly see) is its discontinuity, its suspended uncertainty, with the 'narrative' breaking — or even 'braking' — again and again as though to forestall my suspicions that it might be running downhill. Here, it is the gesture, not movement proper, which reigns. It is the pre-eminence of the gesture — often directed 'against' the camera: e.g. the apostrophizing manual gesticulation (meaning: 'No, don't film me!') by which the face is all but obscured by the magnified palm of the hand in close-up and which is practically a convention (one might say, a cliché) of home movies — that, when surprised (the filmed subject perpetually reacts as though accosted unawares), contrives to *suspend* the feel of duration, exactly as happens in a photograph. One poses, one does not act, for a home movie-maker; or rather, if one does feign to act, for a lark, one's 'performance' remains, as it can never be for the professional actor, a pose. (As one might expect, photography most closely approximates that cinematic suavity mentioned above when the objects of its scrutiny are film stars.)

As for the reciprocal interaction of photography and painting — and beyond the late nineteenth-century influence of camera framing on high art composition, the 'neon-realism' of the American Hyper-Realist school (and some of Pop Art) and the fact that a number of contemporary figurative artists are known to paint from snapshots instead of from life — one has only to consider, precisely, David Hockney's work. With the exception, certainly, of his early prints and paintings (very much the product of a specifically sixties art school mystique, a mystique which has since yielded in glamour to that of the film school) and the celebrated 'swimming pool' series (which provided him, for almost the only time in his career, with not just a subject, 'his' subject, but a purely formal challenge), Hockney's output has differed from photographs mostly on the level of the technical means deployed. He has painted (and here, far from its constituting a criticism, resides the very source of his originality and charm) as though photography had not yet been invented. His oils, watercolours and sketches seem to have been 'taken', snapped — as a painter, he might claim, like his novelist friend Isherwood on the first page of *Goodbye to Berlin*, that 'I am a camera'.

For Hockney, the paintbrush reaffirms itself as what it was, to an extent, prior to the invention of the photographic camera, a recording instrument. And in this, at a period when the great majority of his contemporaries have addressed themselves to more austerely formalist, even abstract, pre-occupations, he is merely reclaiming the lost strategies of high art painting.

Consider his portraiture: languorous young male friends (frequently naked and in bed — the classic homoerotic theme, cynically satirized by Evelyn Waugh in *Decline and Fall*, of the 'sleeping boy'), seemingly oblivious to the artist's presence, 'taken' casually and as though unawares, as in a snapshot or home movie; or acquaintances from the worlds of art and literature, posed slightly more formally yet in repose so ephemeral as to suggest the possibility of Instamatic watercolours; or chummy luminaries from the Anglo-American cultural Establishment (Henry Geldzahler, Sir David Webster, John Kasmin) petrified in the candid, luscious frontality of 'official' photographs (and equally, of course, of the academic portraits by which these have been inspired); or the English dress designer Celia Birtwell, soft, boneless and shimmering, repeatedly and indefatigably sketched in a number of barely differing postures, as though Hockney, mimicking the pseudo-orgasmic chatter of a modish fashion photographer, had been flitting to and fro around her reclining figure and burbling, '*Yes*, darling! That's it! Head maybe just a teensy bit more in profile, love — oh *yes*, hold it like that! Fabulous!' Significantly, too, in his self-portraits, Hockney often portrays himself paint-brush in hand, as though, like a camera, the brush could not help but be *reflected* in the image which it has produced.

Even more apposite, in this respect, are his travel sketches. Hockney is a traveller — or rather, a tourist (he seldom deviates from what one might describe as 'consecrated ground': Fire Island, Vichy, Marrakesh, etc.), and it is with a tourist's acquisitive eye that he observes. In other words, he himself (the peroxide-blond, football-player's-gaudy-striped-shirt, owlish-glasses persona that is his trademark) invariably stamps his own presence on the image, even though out of frame, just as a tourist will photograph the Bridge of Sighs, let's say, or Mount Fuji (of which sites thousands of photographs and postcards already exist) to prove to others, or simply to reassure himself, that *he was there*. What is the true essence of tourism? Paradoxically, the hotel. And, uniquely among those artists who have left us with a pictorial rendering of their peregrinations, Hockney has not shied from including in his vision the hotels in which he and his companions have encamped (St Francis Hotel, San Francisco; Suginoi Hotel, Beppu; Bella Vista Hotel, Macao). On the contrary, they might be said to constitute a recurrent motif (at least since the early cycle of Californian motels), as though what he were concerned to represent were less the 'place' in and of itself than his own brief and uninvolved sojourn in it. And the most affectingly memorable works of all, superbly self-contained and a bit mysterious, confine themselves to evoking the mere *traces* of that sojourn:* a creased white suit and striped tie negligently slung over a wicker chair; a wine glass, a bottle of Vichy water and a Penguin Modern Classic on a restaurant table; three or four spotted bow ties half-obscuring a hotel-room mirror. No

---

* The notion, in art, of the trace, the suspended, still pulsating immobility of a space left vacant, is an intriguing one, as yet insufficiently analysed. I recall, for instance, a photograph which adorned the cover of the English-language edition of Renaud Camus's *Tricks* (an episodic, Calvino-esque account of a sequence of casual homosexual pick-ups to which its author was party) and which depicted a shady, nocturnal, almost spectral, bushy grove in a Parisian park. Though divested of all human presence, it offered an indelible 'afterimage' of furtive liaisons. It should be noted, besides, that what has no doubt remained Hockney's most famous painting to date, 'A Bigger Splash', also happens to be that of a trace.

nineteenth-century traveller, then, is Hockney, but a twentieth-century tourist (his 'China', illustrated in the recently published *China Diary* on which he collaborated with Stephen Spender, is characteristically that which has been 'opened up' to tourism), compelled to paint and sketch what he sees because (as though) the camera, the tourist's Cyclops eye, has yet to find its inventor.

Photography, moreover, is intimately linked to Autobiography: it might be, in effect, the poor man's Memoirs. For what else does one photograph, as though for a localized, *domestic* posterity, but travel, one's wedding, one's wedding anniversaries, the successive stages of a baby's growth, and so forth?

Hockney is, to be sure, far from being the only painter whose output has been informed by discernibly autobiographical elements, but there is, in his case, a crucial distinction to be made. These days the adjective 'autobiographical' − by which art history has commonly denoted the relationship, whether aesthetically transformed or not, between an artist's work and the chronology of his private life − has acquired a strong (socioliterary) connotative value. Autobiography is, in short, and perhaps above all, a literary genre (also audiovisual: e.g. TV 'profiles', film 'biopics'), one which in itself tends to enjoy a greater commercial esteem than the literature whose prominence and reputation prompted its existence in the first place. To take only the most flagrantly obvious, indeed ubiquitous, example − of those countless readers addicted to the autobiographies (and biographies, memoirs, diaries and collected correspondences) of the Bloomsbury set and its raffish fellow-travellers (Virginia and Leonard Woolf, Strachey and Carrington, Vita Sackville-West, Roger Fry, Maynard Keynes, etc.), how many, one wonders, will actually have troubled to *read* the profuse literary outpourings which made them such fascinating and exotic individuals to *read about*? Arguably, it is no longer even a 'life' from which our fascination stems but what is called a 'life-style'. The life of Cecil Beaton, for instance — subject of a detailed bestselling biography and author of a string of name-dropping diaries — was only as dramatic as might be that of any tirelessly energetic photographer, costume designer and social climber. His life-style, on the other hand — a luxuriously febrile whirl of masked balls, house parties, premières, transatlantic voyages and glamorous photo-sessions with royalty, debutantes, Audrey Hepburn and Garbo — could almost have been concocted expressly for a reader to relive by proxy. So it is, too, with the Mitford sisters, Noël Coward, Mick Jagger, whoever — that whole superhuman race with as many biographies to their names as a cat has lives. After all, one scarcely needs to be reminded that Mrs Thatcher is the British Prime Minister: of far more significance to the reader are the furnishings of her neo-Georgian house in Dulwich; and one is well aware that Elvis Presley revitalized American popular music: it is rather his predilection for the spectacle of teenage girls wrestling in their panties which provides the indispensable revelation. (An instance of *pure* life-style, unadulterated by achievement, is granted us by the Princess of Wales.)

And here, I believe, is the source of David Hockney's immense public popularity: not merely the airy, inexhaustible charm of his draughtsmanship and painterliness, but the fact that, by directly transcribing a highly enviable life-style on to canvas, he presents his admirers with, in one handily compact package, the two species of experience through which they have become accustomed to gaining access (if usually by separate channels) to the artistic condition — the aesthetic, naturally, but also the vicarious.

Paedophilia

The public image of sex — in this country, at least — has remained a bizarrely modest one: much spoken about but little seen or, more subtly, felt. (I refer to sex, not nudity, which *has* become increasingly visible.) Notwithstanding the discursive buzz set off by the question on a practically daily basis, there is a pervasive shying away from its strictly biological verities — from, in other words, the trite but stubborn truth that, as Godard has a (female) character rather shockingly remark in one of his films, 'My sexual organs are between my legs.' Let our sexual discourse be medical, political, moral, aesthetic or psychoanalytical (and it is indeed all of these), it is seldom, shall we say, carnal. And deviant sexuality, for its part, is so anxious to maintain a discreet (terrorized?) distance from the erogenic basis of its 'difference' that it has become conceivable, in a sense, to be attracted to one's own sex without quite being 'a homosexual', in the currently accepted connotation of the word. For to be a homosexual now implies that one has assumed an ethics, an aesthetics, a sociopolitical identity, encompassing one's clothes, one's sensibility (usually 'artistic', even camp), one's life-style (there exist gay bars, gay hotels, gay resorts; also gay doctors, gay lawyers, etc.). (That, in statistical terms, such a life-style probably applies to a relatively tiny proportion of homosexuals has in no way diminished its charm as a prototype.) As for the purely physical intercourse of two homosexuals, *as for desire*, it is strangely elsewhere, as though distracted — tangible only in those traces it might have left on their mannerisms, their facial features (their eyes, perhaps). Often portrayed as violent and insatiable in homosexual literature, this desire, in a social framework, is repressed to the point where, as I said, it has become possible to fantasize the whole gay impedimenta of tastes and attitudes as disconnected from the specific sexual orientation from which they are supposed to have derived. It is almost as though male homosexuals kept their genitalia on leads, like small, frisky Pekes; as though it were the Pekes, rather, which met and sniffed each other, while their half mortified, half amused owners stood on the sidelines in poses of slightly studied detachment — saying, 'Oh, you know, it has nothing to do with me.'

Which explains why paedophilia has been thrown into such startling relief. For the paedophiliac, so we are led to believe, has not been blessed with the frivolous conviviality of the homosexual; he (or she) has not, in the absence of a (true, masculine, virile) male, simulated the norms of Judaeo-Christian monogamy, as is said to be the case with lesbians; there is something 'Scandinavian', something nastily, un-Britishly 'Dutch', in the earnestness with which he proselytizes, within ever-contracting legal limits, his formidable otherness.

Of greater significance, however, than the speculative theory that he 'aggresses children' (for not all paedophiliacs are brutal rapists, and children, in any event, are aggressed in so many less publicized ways) is the fact that the only mythology to which he is now entitled is that of his own sexuality, whether crudely or gently exploited. There has long ceased to exist what might be called a paedophiliac sensibility, a paedophiliac camp. The Graeco-Roman cult of such a relationship (exclusively between a man and a boy child, it has to be added), the graceful apologiae of a Wilde, Gide and Montherlant and the endearingly kitschy photographs of the

Baron von Gloeden ('p*ae*dophilia', 'Gr*ae*co-Roman', 'von Gl*oe*den': might there not be *involuntary* signs of ambiguity?) have been engulfed by the indiscriminate shrieks of the tabloid press and the understandable if brazenly manipulated fears of parents. Paedophiliacs, then, are well nigh universally reviled; for them, in a court of law, there can be no mitigating circumstances; and even in prison they must live quarantined from their fellow convicts.

There is no question here of 'defending' paedophilia — merely of indicating just how morally *indispensable* it has become. For in a period when sex strikes the majority of us as bafflingly elusive, maddeningly unmeasurable, and when Good and Evil have so forfeited their immemorial prestige in our eyes that we are far better able to imagine Heaven and Hell as respectively rewarding intelligence and damning stupidity, it does provide an ultimate measure. It is, in short, our sole surviving blasphemy.

The Light Ages

What is truly astonishing about the supernatural these days is the degree to which it is *taken for granted*. For our children, especially, startlingly nimble-fingered at the electronic needlepoint of video games, unfazed by the scariest rides in the cinema's intergalactic funfair, with its vertiginous canyons and dizzy, M. C. Escher-like perspectives (the kitsch of the future), there should scarcely be any difficulty acknowledging Galileo's once heretical blueprint of the universe, according to which the Earth is just one, and not at all the most prominent, of many glistening globes strung up on the cosmic Christmas tree. And presiding over this funfair as ringmaster is the American film-maker Steven Spielberg (of *Close Encounters of the Third Kind*, *E.T.: The Extra-Terrestrial* and others).

There can be attributed to certain major directors a recurrent fetish-image, in which is distilled the essence of their personal mythology — their poetics, if you prefer (Chaplin's was, of course, his climactic trot into the horizon, Woody Allen's might be that of his familiar check-shirted, besneakered and bespectacled person expostulating, gesticulating, with his leading lady on a busy Manhattan street). That of Spielberg — an appropriate motif if ever there was — is of a group of onlookers gazing heavenwards in wonderment (notably, at the Waldorf Astoria chandelier of a spacecraft gravitating to Earth in the final scene of *Close Encounters* and of the prolonged leave-taking of E.T. in his Woolworths' flying-saucer, a very minor piece of extra-terrestrial crockery, indeed). Where, I ask myself, have I already been exposed to such an image (which metaphorically reflects the spectator's own attitude of craning stupefaction when confronted with one of Spielberg's films)? The answer is, in newsreel and photographic footage of Marian (not Martian) visitations. For even if one limits one's data to the present century, it is possible to cite a surprising number of well-documented apparitions of the Virgin, almost invariably to infants or adolescents (precisely Spielberg's public): most recently, at Garabandal in Spain in the early sixties; at Zeitoun, a working-class suburb of Cairo, later in the same decade (snapshots of this apparition, wafting back and forth over a church rooftop, became relatively common); and, concurrently as I write, in the tiny Yugoslav village of Medjugorje. The most stupendous of twentieth-century (Christian) miracles, however, occurred in 1917, in the Portuguese hamlet of Fatima, following a series of Marian visitations to three illiterate peasant children. In the course of one such 'close encounter', the little spokeswoman for the trio, a nine-year-old girl named Lucia dos Santos, requested the Virgin to produce a 'sign' that might convince the sceptics (who included some local Catholic dignitaries). The sign, when it came, was witnessed by a crowd of over seventy thousand people, not all of them devout. And it might be worth quoting at length two first-hand accounts of the event.

Dr Almeida Garete, a professor at the University of Coimbra:

> I was at a distance of little more than a hundred yards away. The rain was pouring down on our heads and, streaming down our clothes, soaked them completely. At last it came along to two o'clock p.m. (official time — really corresponding to noon, solar time). Some instants previously, the

71

radiant sun had pierced the thick curtain of clouds which held it veiled. All eyes were raised towards it as if drawn by a magnet. I myself tried to look straight at it, and saw it looking like a well-defined disc, bright but not blinding. I heard people around me comparing it to a dull silver plate. The comparison did not seem to me exact. Its appearance was of a sharp and changing clarity, like the 'orient' of a pearl. It did not resemble in any way the moon on a fine night. It had neither its colour nor its shadows. You might compare it rather to a polished wheel cut in the silvery valves of a shell. This is not poetry. I saw it thus with my own eyes.

Neither would you confuse it with the sun seen through a fog. Of fog there was no trace, and besides, the solar disc was neither blurred nor veiled in any way, but shone clearly at its centre and at its circumference.

This chequered shining disc seemed to possess a giddy motion. It was not the twinkling of a star. It turned on itself with an astonishing rapidity.

Suddenly a great cry, like a cry of anguish, arose from all this vast throng. The sun with its swiftness of rotation detached itself from the firmament and, blood-red in colour, rushed towards the earth, threatening to crush us under the immense weight of its mass of fire. There were moments of dreadful tension.

All these phenomena, which I have described, I have witnessed personally, coldly and calmly, without the slightest agitation of mind.

And Father Ignatius Lawrence Pereira, who watched the spectacle as a child from his schoolroom approximately nine miles away:

Our teacher rushed out, and the children all ran after her.

In the public square people wept and shouted, pointing to the sun, without paying the slightest heed to the questions of our teacher: it was the great solar prodigy with all its wonderful phenomena which was seen distinctly even from the hill on which my village was situated. This miracle I feel incapable of describing such as I saw it at that moment. I looked fixedly at the sun, which appeared pale and did not dazzle. It looked like a ball of snow turning on itself . . . Then suddenly it seemed to become detached from the sky, and rolled right and left, as if it were falling upon the earth. Terrified, absolutely terrified, I ran towards the crowd of people. All were weeping, expecting at any moment the end of the world.

During the long minutes of the solar phenomena, the objects around us reflected all the colours of the rainbow. Looking at each other, one appeared blue, another yellow, a third red, etc., and all these strange phenomena only increased the terror of the people. After about ten minutes the sun climbed back into its place, as it had descended, still quite pale and without brilliance.

When the people were convinced that the danger had passed, there was an outburst of joy.*

If I might do so without any disrespect to its witnesses (for, whatever actually happened at Fatima, it was no 'vision': seventy thousand people, not a few of them from outlying regions, cannot be collectively hypnotized), I should call this strange 'dance of the sun' Spielbergian or para-Spielbergian: not only in its spectacle, in its suspense and in the ineffable sweetness of its resolution, but in relation to the way the director has appropriated, streamlined and secularized a whole, primitively traditionalist Catholic iconography, of a type identified by the French as 'Saint-

*These testimonies are extracted from William T. Walsh's study *Our Lady of Fatima*.

Sulpician'. Thus, where the Virgin communes with the most untutored and uncorrupt of her subjects, children, so it is the younger generation from whose ranks are enlisted not merely the most devoted (and cyclical) section of Spielberg's audience but, in the films themselves, the only characters capable of entering into a guileless and unapprehensive communication with alien beings: e.g. *E.T.*'s Elliott, whose empathetic affinity with the forlorn extra-terrestrial is signalled by the detail that his name, too, is book-ended by E and T; or the child Barry (a name to be read as symbolically homophonic with that of [J.M.] Barrie ?), who is whisked aloft in the spacecraft of *Close Encounters*. While the Marian visitations are concentrated on rural, piously Catholic communities (where, oddly, she tends to materialize either on top of, or just beyond, a hillock situated some few hundred yards outside the village in question), Spielberg's 'Martian' wayfarers (here, it has to be said, respecting a tradition of much Hollywood science-fiction) analogously orient themselves towards the pleasantly standardized small towns, suburbs and shopping malls of the American hinterland. Moreover, the most frequent 'by-products' of religious visions (solar phenonema, stigmata, levitation, etc.) also have their equivalents in the film-maker's suburban Arcadia (Barry's mechanical toys mysteriously whirring into life, 'demonstrating themselves', as it were, across his bedroom rug as though on the floor of some department store showroom; in the same film, nimbus clouds forming, unforming and re-forming, boiling and curdling at the spacecraft's passage, in a style recalling the delightful illustrations of the East Wind and the West Wind in picture-books from our childhood; and, in *E.T.*, when Elliot and his chums join forces to deliver their wizened foundling from the vivisectionary ambitions of his adult tormentors, the magical shot of their bikes becoming unceremoniously airborne).

I might add, finally, that it is as true of cinematic special effects as of miracles themselves: abuse or overuse of them, while furthering their credibility as objective phenomena, paradoxically compromises the spectator's credence in their *implications*, in the existence of a 'higher' form of being (higher in both altitude and attitude) of which they are but the naive manifestations. In fact, and belying his reputation, Spielberg deploys special effects with an admirable economy (in *E.T.*, particularly, where, save for its purely ludic applications, technology is made the sole preserve of what subsists of the malignant 'Other': i.e., the grown-up).

As one knows, science-fiction bears exactly the same relation to the future, or to any of the planet's foreseeable futures as fairy-tales do to the (crypto-medieval) past. In both genres, for instance, animals (or robots and aliens*) have been invested with the at present exclusively human attributes of rational thought and speech; the control systems, laser rays, microchips and ultrasounds of science-fiction — the whole dazzling cascade of what might be called (after Dufy) *la fée électronique* — constitute a vertiginous new alchemy, a Faustian, near-infinite fund of knowledge and power; and one immediately recognizes in both the same narrative structures, the same Manichaean confrontations, the same elemental themes of apprenticeship, quest and redemption. It is almost as though, for writers and film-makers of science-fiction, the Earth were (eternally) poised on the brink of a kind of Light Ages — a 'positive' reprint of the Dark.

With Spielberg, however — and Stanley Kubrick was his prophet — the genre has now acquired a candidly uplifting vocation: he is clearly groping towards a literal *theology* of Space, Christian and New Testament-based in its specifics

---

*Aliens are now being used, as formerly were animals, to add 'human interest' to a film.

(whereas Kubrick's 'godhead', the black monolith of *2001*, was in essence an Old Testament icon, cold, smooth, seamless, inhumanly un-orificed, and only obliquely communicative). It is in Spielberg's films, too, that one can locate not only the (apparently) impregnable optimism of science-fiction but trace the distance it has covered since its baptism in the Industrial Revolution: from a faith in the future to, currently, the unfashionable belief — one, after all, inherent in the genre — that there will be a future at all. And since these films are predicated on a universe of infinite spiritual consciousness, one in which the most advanced physics at last achieves total harmony with a demonstrably metaphysical system, one might well be tempted to regard such faith as of a genuinely 'religious' order — Christian science-fiction, in other words.

S/he

Throughout this section of the book (of which the essay you are about to read is, as though by chance, situated exactly at the halfway point) I have used the masculine 'he' to designate, without further distinction, any indeterminate human referent ('the reader', 'the viewer' and so forth) whose gender happens to be immaterial: the 'he', in other words, of what most of us are still accustomed to calling '*man*kind'. Naturally, I am aware that a grammatical formula enabling one to circumvent the ostensible sexism of that immemorial convention has recently been devised: to wit, 's/he'. Yet I have consciously rejected the usage — though I am not averse to the more cumbrous, if more elegant, 'he or she' insofar as the context seems to demand such a precision of imprecision, so to speak. Am I, then, wittingly or unwittingly, a sexist writer?

The stake is less frivolous than might at first appear. The grand, liberating causes of feminism having been won, lost or else abandoned (temporarily, one hopes) by weary campaigners anxious to 'get on with their lives', the crusade has centred on certain localized raids, notably on the male-controlled citadel of language: I refer to the (possibly Pyrrhic) victories of 'Ms', 'chairperson' (not to mention that somewhat sinister Orwellianism, the *ex post facto* revision of 'Weathermen' into 'Weatherpersons') and 's/he'. There is no question but that language is still a male preserve on the whole, a clubby enclave within which the presence of women is at best suffered, usually gladly. Or that the problem of a truly feminine (as distinct from feminist)* literature is a genuine, enduring and perhaps even insoluble one. So that, should a male writer (myself, for instance) complain that the systematic use of 's/he', however progressive, would deface the layout of his text with infelicitous slash marks, a feminist might reasonably argue that, by this means at least, her sex has contrived to get a foot in the door of language, an affair of greater significance, when all is said and done, than the gratification of typographical vanity. So be it. I have, on principle, no objection to such an argument. Nor would it occur to me to raise the spectre of 'jargon': every language is a jargon before it becomes a language; and our language, i.e. that which currently represents the lexical, grammatical and rhetorical pool of our every discourse, whether written or oral, is nothing but the encrustation and imbrication of jargon upon jargon (sociopolitical, technological, psychoanalytical, vernacular, whatever) over the years.

It nevertheless remains true that I have an almost intestinal distaste for the locution — a distaste deriving, however, from my sympathy with the women's movement. Without in any way subscribing to the received idea of feminists as dour, humourless, embittered hybrids — failures, somehow, as both women *and* men — still, I do find myself compelled to acknowledge the fact that the movement (like most forms of militancy, male or female) has generated in its wake a slight coarsening of the intelligence, what one might describe as a *strategic* stupidity. (As men should know, one has to be 'stupid' to fight a battle but intelligent to win it.) For how, otherwise, could feminists have failed to comprehend that, in this insistence upon 's/he', they risk surrendering what is potentially one of the sharpest instruments of linguistic

---

*And beyond such dog-eared stereotypes of the feminine sensibility as 'delicacy', 'fragility' and 'grace'.

subversion at their disposal. The 'he' which has historically predominated in written and spoken English is not 'masculine' but 'neuter' (or rather, neutral); it embraces, indiscriminately, men and women; which now means that 'man' tends to imply 'mankind', not (as feminists would have it) vice versa. Prior to a baby's birth, for instance, it is commonly alluded to as 'he' (and, of course, as witness this very sentence of mine, 'it'). It has therefore a purely existential, rather than sexual, identity. Once born, should it happen to be a boy, it cannot help but retain that neutrality of gender (linguistically speaking); whereas, if a girl, it enters the world with not only a name but an autonomously determined sexual identity: *she*. 'She' designates a woman, 'he' a person; 'she' is particular, 'he' is general; 'she' is someone, 'he' is anyone.

The Playboy of the West End

If I were to simplify, I might propose that the difference between Pinter's plays and those of Stoppard is that, whereas the former make the spectator feel (temporarily) stupid, the latter make him feel (temporarily) intelligent. This difference derives from two radically divergent conceptions of how language best functions in the theatre: whether, and again to simplify, one is left aching to *turn the meaning up*, as one adjusts the volume control on a radio (Pinter), or *down* (Stoppard).

In Pinter's case, the oddity of his jarring yet somehow eerily serene rhythms recalls the (unnamed?) party game in which one answers not one's own designated question but that posed immediately before it — as well as the solipsistic paranoia both exemplified and parodied by the formula 'I know that you know that I know . . .' So magisterially self-sufficient is the result that *mise en scène*, performers and even, so to speak, one's own physical presence in the auditorium end by effacing themselves before a text which thereby, paradoxically, re-attains the ideogrammatic 'virginity' of its pre-theatrical existence on the printed (or manuscript) page. And whether there is more or less to Pinter's ambiguously bourgeois, proscenium-arch dramas than meets the eye (and ear) — though a matter of vital and often reiterated concern to his exegetes — may, in the final analysis, be of lesser significance than the vertiginous capacity of his spoken dialogue to distanciate itself from its own representational context.

Where Pinter's language may be said to generate situations, however, the reverse is true of Stoppard's (as witness the intellectuality with which he routinely invests his protagonists, from Joyce, Lenin and Tristan Tzara to philosophers, playwrights, journalists and drama critics, an intellectuality prompted by his own natural tendency to linguistic pyrotechnics); and where Pinter's language is entirely the product of a 'construction', Stoppard's is 'sincere' (a term employed by Barthes to define the commensurately verbal theatre of Jean Giraudoux, Stoppard's predecessor): which is to say, the permanent sense of language *showing off*, sporting its Sunday best, as it were, is perceived as a faithful echo of the dramatist's own celebrated braininess, being theatricalized only to the degree that it has been heightened, optimized, purged of those 'miscues', those anxiety-inducing dislocations of meaning (and that generate another meaning altogether, as in the game mentioned above) out of which, precisely, Pinter articulates his plays.

Stoppard's language would appear to be aware of a single mode of expression: that of *brio*. His plays 'dazzle', they stimulate us with 'firework displays of verbal ingenuity' they take our breath away with their 'inexhaustible linguistic richness' — to borrow from the inventorial, handily quoteful idiom of the popular press. True enough; but, as one of his own characters might well retort, 'to dazzle' means also 'to blind', only monosyllabic messages can adequately be conveyed by fireworks, and the artists who are deemed richest tend to be those with a lot of small change jangling in their pockets. As a practice, of course, such fidgety fragmentation, the volatilizing of a work of art into apparently disconnected particles of meaning (expressed, here, in puns, jokes, literary conceits and elaborately spiralling flights of fancy), is by no means questionable in itself: not for nothing was an intricately multifaceted period of Cubism named Analytical.

81

But it may equally constitute — and, I believe, does in Stoppard's case — a form of mystification. 'Deconstructing a text', or merely dismantling its narrative linearity: these are, to be sure, strategies central to modernism. Yet, in the cycle of political thrillers directed by Francesco Rosi (*Lucky Luciano, The Mattei Affair* etc.), in which can be detected similar procedures, the spectator, bombarded (as in a 3-D film) with glinting slivers of information but deprived of the opportunity of intelligibly recombining them, leaves the cinema with a complacently fascinated, therefore *mystified*, vision of Italian politics, the Mafia or whatever as configurations of power and evil so elusively complex, tentacular and Byzantine as to defy all hope of his ever understanding them. And the same is true, setting aside differences of subject-matter, of Stoppard's work.

Consider what is perhaps the wittiest and most skilful of his plays, *Travesties* (whose unflagging drollery it would be churlish and perverse to deny). Certainly, the basic narrative is a prodigy of eccentric speculation. Playing Algernon Moncrieff in an amateur production of *The Importance of Being Earnest*, Henry Carr, a minor official at the British consulate in Zurich during the First World War (and an individual who existed in reality), becomes embroiled with a trio of the century's most notorious geniuses, each of them a prominent avant-gardist in his respective field and all of them, by one of history's agreeable accidents, also domiciled in Zurich in 1917: Joyce, Lenin and Tristan Tzara. And the play might be summed up as a Wildean fantasia on the three weighty artistic and political movements which have attached to their now famous names: literary modernism, revolutionary Marxism and Dada. The fact that Stoppard's dialogue abounds in puns and surreal non-sequiturs not only confirms, in the public's mind, his own pyrotechnical gifts, it permits him to appropriate Joyce and Tzara as his intellectual peers and predecessors. This is what I meant by the 'sincerity' of his language, whose brilliance — validated, even redeemed, by the hyper-intellectual status of its subjects — can hence be acquitted *in extremis* of the charge (a serious one in the context of the British theatre) of stylization and meekly brought back into the fold of naturalism. Where Lenin is concerned, however — a personage, after all, to whom it would be impossible, 'sincerely' (realistically), to ascribe such an orgy of punnilingus — Stoppard simply abdicates his responsibility as a creator. He makes no attempt to construct what might have been the language of the private Lenin, preferring to extract it piecemeal from his Collected Writings. The character consequently exercises none of the dramatic (or comedic) authority with which Stoppard has endowed his two fellow-revolutionaries — a significant structural flaw.

Even more significant, though, is the way in which the play — quite purposely, it would appear — travesties* its protagonists. Tzara, first of all: when the curtain rises, he is installed in the Zurich Public Library cutting a text up into strips and depositing the fragments in his hat (i.e. as everyone knows, the Dadaists invented the cut-up technique of literary composition); the word Dada is used as little more than a source of (fairly puerile) punning on the order of '. . . my art belongs to Dada 'cos Dada 'e treats me so well . . .' and '. . . my brother has been a great disappointment to me, and to Dada. His mother isn't exactly mad about him either' (i.e. as its self-adopted name suggests, Dada was essentially frivolous); reference is made in passing to a 'noise concert for siren, rattle and fire extinguisher' (i.e. all modern art is charlatanry); and the ideological contradiction inherent in every systematized form of anarchism is encapsulated in a flippantly brief exchange between Carr and Tzara:

*That *Travesties* is its (ambiguous) title is neither here nor there.

83

    CARR: I don't think there'll be a place for Dada in a Communist society.

    TZARA: That's what we have against this one. There's a place for us in it.

Joyce comes off worse. He wears jackets and pairs of trousers from different and mismatching suits (i.e. though a pauper, he had sartorial pretensions); he speaks almost exclusively in limericks (i.e. the Irish — or Oirish — are, as we know, obsessed with wordplay); the novel on which he is labouring is alluded to at one point as *Elasticated Bloomers* (i.e. instantly identifiable as the 'unreadable' *Ulysses*, with its monstrous puns, its protagonist, Leopold Bloom, its juicy bits); and so forth.

What do the above parenthetical inserts represent? A kitty of received ideas concerning Joyce and Tzara: whatever, so to speak, is already *in the public domain*. And if a spectator should chance to enter the theatre burdened with such prejudices, they are likely to have remained intact and, indeed, been reinforced by the time he leaves it; certainly, nothing in the play will have invited him to revise them. In a general manner — and given how caricaturally sectarian it has been rendered — all intellectual exploration becomes the butt of Stoppard's quick-witted sarcasm, as in one speech which 'defends' Marxist orthodoxy by way of a tongue-twisting litany of splinter groups reminiscent of nothing so much as a Danny Kaye scat song:

The only way is the way of Marx, and of Lenin, the enemy of all revisionism — of economism — opportunism — liberalism — of bourgeois anarchist individualism — of quasi-socialist ad hoc-ism, of syndicalist quasi-Marxist populism — liberal quasi-communist opportunism, economist quasi-internationalist imperialism, social chauvinist quasi-Zimmervaldist Menshevism, self-determinist quasi-socialist annexationism, Kautskyism, Bundism, Kantism –

Everything is cause for a giggle – everything, that is, except the obstinately inflexible figure of Lenin. Lenin *eludes* Stoppard, in the sense that he resists being incorporated into the cod Wildean scheme of the play – no doubt because the enduring consequences of Marxism-Leninism as a praxis (consequences to which the dramatist, of Czech origin, may be especially sensitive and of which, in any case, no middle-class West End audience needs to be reminded) preclude his being dismissed as a perpetrator of absurdist hoaxes, as an *aberration*. Unable to dramatize Lenin's history, Stoppard proceeds to serve it up raw, theatrically undigested, in the shape of a lengthy, frankly pedagogic lecture, over which there hovers an invisible schoolmaster's pointer. It starts thus:

It was with considerable surprise that Marx learned of the Russian translation of *Das Kapital*. This appeared in St Petersburg in 1872, before being translated into any other language. He didn't know what to make of it. The conditions for a socialist revolution as he saw it did not exist in Russia at all. Two thirds of the population were peasants, the industrial age had hardly begun, and the proletariat was correspondingly insignificant. According to Marxist theory Russia still had to pass through the whole bourgeois-capitalist cycle.

As one may observe, anyone at all informed in the rudiments of twentieth-century political history could, without risk to his comprehension of the plot, slip out of the auditorium during this speech to smoke a cigarette in the foyer.

Is there, however, a subtext, as one says, another, more profound level on which *Travesties* produces and disseminates meaning? No doubt: if the play is 'about' something, then it is about the ideological relativity of radicalism in all its various manifestations and the near-impossibility of reconciling — rather, of *synchronizing* — the radicalist impulse in art (inherently elitist and recondite) with that in politics (inherently egalitarian and positivist). Yet what these two layers of significance together resemble are those of a box of chocolates — the lower, 'deeper' layer reveals itself on examination to be only a rearrangement of the upper. A comedy (when not, precisely, the exceptional case of *The Importance of Being Earnest* — but one should never take an exception as an example) draws what subversive, liberating force it might possess from its capacity to partake of its subject's emotional, intellectual or even negativist charge at the same time as it is being mocked. *Travesties*, though, has no such power to liberate, having chosen for subjects two (as it views them) figures of fun (*nowhere* does the play directly or indirectly acknowledge their fundamental seriousness) whom it then, rather redundantly, ridicules — at best a tautological exercise, at worst a terrorist one.

But then, as Barthes wrote, 'any reservation about culture is a terrorist position'. Which is what, finally, makes Stoppard such a bizarre figure. With *Travesties* (as well as with *Rosencrantz and Guildenstern Are Dead*, *The Real Inspector Hound*, *Jumpers*, *The Real Thing*, etc.) he escorts consenting West End audiences into a world to which, were he almost any other dramatist, they would have to be dragged kicking and screaming: the wonderful world of ideas. By parodying or travestying these ideas, he demonstrates the superior agility of his own intellect; and by focusing his audience's attention on the parody, at the expense of the ideas which inspired it, he affords it the illusion (for two-and-a-half hours) of being mentally as agile as he himself (Stoppard's theatre is illusionistic with a vengeance). Whereupon, he snaps his fingers; and, as though aroused from a collective hypnosis, the audience files out of the theatre, no wiser than when it entered. Stoppard is, in fact, the contrary of a vulgarizer: he is a genuine intellectual, except that what he intellectualizes is anti-intellectualism.

Wimbledon

Wimbledon, as a spectacle and a competition, incorporates numerous elements from the iconography of the Court: it has never betrayed what we know to have been the *royal* origins of tennis (in the Jeu de Paume). But how exactly was life at court organized? For anyone not a historian, what scant acquaintance (vicarious acquaintance) one can claim with such an existence most likely derives from a few historical films, which have tended to concentrate on its privileged moments of crisis and festivity. Thus, in the first instance (crisis), the King, wearing something akin to a bejewelled medieval ashtray on his head and attended by twin rows of courtiers (traditionally aligned parallelwise on either side of the throne), would be shown granting audience to a messenger from the field of battle, let's say, or a treaty-bearing emissary from a neighbouring kingdom; in the second (festivity), the same King and courtiers would be seen, on the occasion of a royal wedding or some comparable ceremony, being entertained by singing and dancing, jousting and, indeed, tennis-playing. One cannot help but wonder, however, what happened between these fitful excitements. The monarch, naturally, would confer with his council of ministers – but what, meanwhile, did his courtiers do? Play cards? Patiently or impatiently bide their time until an emissary's arrival? Count the months between royal weddings? Though court memoirists have understandably opted to narrate the more eventful aspects of their experience, one can nevertheless deduce that the essence of such quotidian court attendance, as of its contemporary avatars (garden-parties, private views), was a faintly enervating sense of boredom edgily tempered by a reluctance to absent oneself and risk missing something.

There, too, is the essence of the Wimbledon experience. To be sure, one watches the Championship (and I am referring here to its television coverage) for the sheer brilliance of the sport; in the hope, too, of a startling reversal of fortune (an increasingly rare occurrence these days, what with the matchless virtuosity of three or four top-seeded players: in consequence, all the more thrilling when it does occur, e.g. the young Boris Becker's victory in 1985); and finally — naggingly — because during the fortnight in which the event unfolds, and no matter how predictable it might appear to have become (particularly where the women's matches are concerned), one simply refuses to admit the possibility of tearing oneself away, of not *being there*.

This rather schizophrenic or 'amletico' (from the Italian word for 'Hamlet') dilemma -- to stay (tuned) or not to stay — is intensified by the fact that, in its presentation of Wimbledon, the BBC does not merely content itself with reporting those moments of highest energy and suspense but quite consciously seeks to convey the event's decorous, well nigh unvarying yet still nostalgically charming connective tissue.

There are, to begin with, all kinds of obvious, even nominal analogies with the minutiae of a royal court (that, for instance, of its *locus classicus*, Louis XIV's Versailles): the term 'court' itself; the physical presence of royalty (Wimbledon's patrons are the Duke and Duchess of Kent); the consumption of such 'patrician' delicacies as strawberries and champagne; the well-drilled palace guard of umpires, linesmen, and so on (formerly open to charges of snoozing on the job, like some old court retainer played by Sir C. Aubrey Smith in a Hollywood film); the aristocratic stylization of the sport's gestuality (McEnroe's graceful curtsey as he prepares to serve, Navratilova's nimble follow-up dash to the net); and the arcane, 'undecimalized' scoring notation (love, 15, 30, 40, deuce, etc.), preserved from the original Jeu de Paume. Wimbledon equally reveals its basic (and sometimes pompous and off-putting) passéism in the fact that it remains one of the very few major tournaments to be contested on a grass surface, on that still potent signifier of both old-world Englishness and ingrained amateurism, a *lawn*. The economic foundation of that amateurism may have been overtaken by the huge profits to be reaped, by players and entrepreneurs alike, on the international tennis circuit, but its signifier is, from an ideological standpoint, as operational as ever. By the same token, the clay surface of the Roland Garros stadium in which the French Championship is held might be viewed as a sign of professionalism and that, completely synthetic, of New York's Flushing Meadow, of commercialization. (These are, it should be understood, *signified* values, not necessarily legitimate ones.) Finally (here combining with the iconography of the Quest — implicit in every competition whose contestants advance by way of a series of ritual 'ordeals' towards an ultimate, cherished objective, a Grail: in this case, the male champion's gold cup or the plate which enhaloes, Madonna-like, the female champion as she raises it above her head for the benefit of press photographers), there is the patent affinity of tennis with jousting: in the cut-and-thrust of a rally; the decisive, 'mortal' blow represented by a service ace; and the delicious paroxysm of those (alas, all too infrequent) instants at which the two players simultaneously approach the net and, without its ever touching the ground, the ball rebounds briskly, and more or less horizontally, off one racquet straight on to the other.

In its pre-media period, as a competition only,

Wimbledon was more or less exclusively reserved for those select few wealthy or lucky enough to be able to attend the event in person. It is, however, with the BBC's annual television coverage that the Championship has attained its plenitude as a spectacle, as a 'court' (since Louis XIV, a royal court has almost invariably constituted a spectacle, stage-managed for the delectation — which is to say, the benign or malign oppression — of 'the people', cf. Rossellini's *La Prise du pouvoir par Louis XIV*), a shift in emphasis relegating the spectators inside the stadium, as henceforth an integral part of that spectacle (the TV cameras will occasionally flash a shot of some prominent figure glimpsed among the crowd), to the status of 'extras' or courtiers. Even if, to be sure, newspapers provide us during the competition with daily accounts of the state of play (in the 'qualities') and the players' moods, tantrums and private lives (in the tabloids), they are inherently unqualified to do justice to its *textures*, its courtly 'feel' — which remains the province of television. So that it is wholly consistent with what Wimbledon has become that its participants, like young knights at a medieval court, display on their sportswear the 'colours', not of a Queen or lady-in-waiting, but of the product by which, in exchange for extensive 'free' publicity, their ambitions have been sponsored.

The role to which we, the television viewers, are assigned in this royal *fête champêtre* is an ambiguous one. We are, as might be expected, 'the people', fascinated not simply by the spectacle of our betters at play but also by the quite mesmeric intensity which tennis acquires on the small screen: image-wise, in the metronomic oscillation, back and forth from player to player, of spectators' heads; sound-wise, in the rhythmic thwack of the ball as it bounds from one half of the court to the other: two classic feints of the hypnotist. Yet because, paradoxically, it is in the medium's very nature to undercut that fascination — through an audiovisual encrustation of statistics, commentaries, action replays and interviews – we become courtiers as well, and privileged ones in relation to those spectators who have secured stadium seats: not only because of the overview accorded us (and of which, as I have tried to show, they themselves form a constituent element) but because of the ceremonious, even noble, style in which the event is communicated to us by television.

That job lot of writers who pass, in the Sunday newspapers, for TV critics (and who are neurotically preoccupied with Wimbledon) take a malicious pleasure in mimicking the commentaries of Dan Maskell, his impetuous and chivalrous 'Oh, I say!'s and indiscriminate superlatives. But what is significant about Maskell's mannerisms is the degree to which he has remained an appropriately 'amateur', i.e. aristocratic, chronicler, to the point where it is hard to credit his being paid for speaking as he does. We do not hear his commentary, we 'overhear' it, as we might overhear some eloquent and enthusiastic spectator seated in a box adjacent to our own. He is, if you like, Wimbledon's old retainer, who knows everything, has seen everything yet has not ceased to be amazingly unblasé. And if Maskell is the event's breezy memoirist, its Saint-Simon, then it is the medium of television itself (if I may be permitted to jumble different periods together) which is its audiovisual troubadour. Television, in other words, *sings* Wimbledon, its song or 'lay' now polyphonic, now fugal: e.g. the unchanging, endlessly reiterated angles of vision; the periodic insertion of a high-angle shot over the stadium; and the affecting manner in which an action replay instantly transforms the present into the past and, by a use of slow motion that is both functional and sublime though rarely sentimental, lends it an *epic* dimension.

Watching a football match, by contrast, the TV viewer finds himself forced into a kind of tunnel vision. Outside of the pitch itself, its play of action and counteraction, there is nothing, a void. His scrutiny focuses indivisibly on twenty-two players, a referee and a ball. The crowd is merely that, a crowd perceived *en bloc*, the textural trappings are minimal and the game soon settles into its quasi-permanent state of crisis, violence and suspense. In short, it constitutes not an event but a conflict, not a court but a battlefield.

By one of those brilliantly glib locutions which he was able to formulate at will, Marshall McLuhan enriched the language with the concept of 'the global village', thereby casting television in the role of newsy postmistress or switchboard operator, the vital juncture through which an entire circuit of information is obliged to pass. In a similarly hyperbolic spirit (and given its unrivalled viewing figures throughout the world), one might regard Wimbledon — at least, Brigadoon-like, for fourteen days in the year — as the global Camelot.

Dr Barnardo's Orphans

One knows the importance assumed since the Romantic period, and in particular during the late nineteenth century, by the Child. Childhood, from having been judged neither more nor less than a waste of time, to be matured out of as swiftly as possible, began instead to be perceived as a kind of Rousseauist idyll, a halcyon isle of purity and innocence far removed from the malign mainland of adult society. In this sense, the orphan constituted the very essence of childhood, since he or she had even been deprived of the contagion of normal (or abnormal) family routine. The prominence accorded to the orphan by nineteenth-century novelists — not only Dickens, not only in this country — became in consequence rather hypertrophied when compared to his actual footing on the social hierarchy, both qualitatively and quantitatively; and, in a much-quoted witticism from *The Importance of Being Earnest* (Lady Bracknell's observation that the loss of both parents resembled 'carelessness'), Wilde, no devotee of Dickensian sentimentality, mocked what might be called the rampant orphanomania of the Victorians. (His attitude to the widow, infallibly twinned with the orphan, was not less cynical.)

What, then, has become of the orphan? Demographically, it is a vanishing breed, an endangered species, as one says these days. Without — in the Western hemisphere, at least — the great epidemic calamities of war and disease, there are no longer, as previously, 'waves' of orphaned children; which means that, in the wake of the Second World War, the word has acquired a 'foreign', fundamentally Third World, connotation (Korean orphans, Vietnamese orphans). Our collective national conscience tends to ignore its own orphans, who impinge upon it less through the continuing efforts than through the name itself, a vividly evocative one, of Dr Barnardo's Homes. In recent years, like some American conglomerate, Barnardo's Homes have considerably diversified their charitable preoccupations: the orphan, however, remains the trademark of the organization, and his plaster effigy (beside that of the good Dr himself, the epitome of a Victorian philanthropist, with his pince-nez, his fob watch and his *embonpoint*) is still to be seen on the doorsteps of old-fashioned chemist shops. Yet (and I intend no disrespect to the children themselves, it being solely their public image with which I am concerned) there now strikes one as something dated and irreducibly kitschy about an orphan: a Barnardo Boy reminds one of nothing so much as a Bisto Kid. In effect, the social specificity of a nineteenth-century orphan was contingent upon an uncompromisingly normative conception of society, from which he was therefore − if in this manner alone − *not* alienated, since he had been assigned a codified place within it, however luckless. Today, when the notion of a society regulated by an exclusive set of ideological criteria has forfeited much of its authority, and when what would have been regarded until quite lately as unimaginable anomalies compete with each other for the attention of the sociologist, the social worker and the investigative journalist (single-parent families, lesbian mothers, test-tube babies), the orphan has lost not only his parents but his *status*.

La Dame aux Gladioli

It is one of the minor malaises of contemporary alienation to feel that one has come *after*, that one was born *too late*. Are you travelling to Paris or Vienna? Then someone will inevitably advise you that neither Paris nor Vienna is what it used to be. You are interested in the arts? Invariably, the period you traverse turns out to be, at best, one of synthesis, at worst, of stagnation. The French Riviera has been ruined by tourists and caravan sites, not one of the great and glamorous Tangerine expatriates continues to inhabit Tangiers, Sutherland is as nothing compared to Flagstad, and Olivier a poor man's Irving or Forbes-Robertson − the refrain is a tediously familiar one. It is, therefore, with untempered enthusiasm that I should like to celebrate a currently peforming artist who strikes me as representing the very consummation of an aesthetics which has been notoriously prey to this brand of nostalgic intimidation: that of the music hall. I mean, Dame Edna Everage, Housewife-Superstar (alias the Australian humorist Barry Humphries).

The initial paradox of Dame Edna's act is that it does not in any way exploit the mythology of the transvestite. Curiously, one of the few sociopsychic tensions which 'she' (and from here on I shall omit the inverted commas) refrains from capitalizing on is that of cross-dressing; and if there is a conspicuous absentee from the show − even from the theatre's traditional 'midnight', the moment of its unmasking, i.e. the curtain call − it is Barry Humphries himself. Though, during a typical performance, Humphries will incarnate several different characters (the most memorable of which, apart from Dame Edna, being Sir Les Patterson, Australia's self-presumed 'Minister of Culture', an oafishly disgusting *bon vivant* whose crotch, when he sits down, reminds one of a battleship being launched), each of these remains a wholly discrete creation, both from one another and from its (as I say, invisible) creator. In Dame Edna's case, the justification for such absolute self-containment seems clear: the primary relationship by which the show is articulated is that forged between the public and herself, the (quite literal) tensions generated throughout the evening are those which flow between the auditorium and the stage, from the latter of which a total self-confidence must therefore radiate. Enveloped in her platitudes and prejudices, oblivious to the merest twinge of self-doubt, Dame Edna is the least *ambiguous* of women.

Another paradox: it is precisely in the progressive inflation of her personal identity that one can locate the true value of her act. When she made her first appearances some twenty years ago in Australia, Dame Edna's name was not as prestigiously prefixed as it was later to become, nor had the honorific 'Superstar' yet been appended to 'Housewife'. However, just as bigoted, credulous and *petite-bourgeoise* then as now, her discourse an insidiously bubbly stream of old and new wives' tales, populist cant phrases and received widsom, she regularly courted the risk (as did 'Alf Garnett' in the BBC TV situation comedy series *Till Death Us Do Part*) of enlisting covert allies and partisans who were either insensitive to, or purposely disregarded, the satirical foundation of her rhetoric. Since when, her career has known an astonishing growth. With increasing international success, she has expanded into a monster of gaudily stylized vulgarity and philistinism. Her prejudices have also become, significantly, monstrous and stylized — so much so, in effect, that *every member of the audience can now plainly see them for what they are.* In short, it is unthinkable that anyone could now wish to identify with her.

Rendering still more unlikely any complacent, half-amused acquiescence in her bloated truisms of race and class is the fact that these are never addressed 'sideways', so to speak, to a comparably larger-than-life character on stage, but directly to us (or to our neighbours) in the auditorium. When she insistently flutters a red handkerchief at a Pakistani spectator, for instance, accompanying her gesture with the racist commonplace that 'our swarthy brothers often respond to bright colours', or derides the flat South London vowel sounds of some equally hapless victim, it could not be more forcefully impressed upon us that each of us is another's 'Other' whose social, racial and physical traits, to which we ourselves tend to be fairly inattentive, make us no less vulnerable to prejudice. What Dame Edna does best is *divide* an audience (a familiar technique of totalitarian oppression): it is each man for himself; one becomes, as rarely in the theatre, an individual surrounded by individuals. And, at the risk of trivializing the concept, I would call the act truly cathartic, in the sense that the emotions it arouses are the classic Aristotelian duality of pity and terror: pity for those unfortunate members of the audience — *nos semblables, nos frères* — who find themselves apostrophized, harangued, humiliated and, eventually, hauled on to the stage by this flamboyant one-off clone; and terror, of course, at the notion that we ourselves might subsequently be subjected to her odious attentions. There is a whiff of sulphur in the air. One laughs, to be sure (Humphries, I should mention, is a brilliantly funny writer and performer), but as excruciatingly as though one were being tickled. Though it is firmly anchored in a music-hall tradition, there is a terrorist dimension to the act which relates it to what used to be called the Theatre of Cruelty: Dame Edna is the sole offspring of Artaud and Max Miller. In fact, Humphries' method is the contrary of Brecht's — not so much a 'distanciation effect' as an 'intensification effect', one that turns the stage into an enormous magnifying glass in which all our prejudices, our stale stereotypes and latent squalors are mercilessly exposed.

This, then, is the grandeur of Dame Edna Everage: fusing the psychic (a variation on the age-old nightmare of finding oneself unclothed in a public place) with the ideological, she liberates whatever is 'repressed' in us by the sanest possible agency: that of laughter. And we shall be able to tell *our* grandchildren, and all those who were born *too late*, how privileged we were to have seen her in person.

Common Places

It is a strange fact that, for newspapers, the theme of the voyage (by which word is intended not so much an ocean journey as the enduring essence of all travel) is generally confined to the winter months. It is as though, beyond the calendrical seasons, the rhythm of the years were regulated pendulum-style, from Christmas on one side to high summer on the other, with everything between these two privileged moments of our existence consigned to pallid abstraction. And, as October infallibly finds us outraged by the first precocious signs of Christmas in department store display windows, so, at the onset of the New Year, colour supplements are suddenly concerned to draw our attention, with a kind of dreamy urgency, to the white beaches of the Caribbean and the châteaux of the Loire, to the modest pros and rather more formidable cons of Aeroflot and the ambiguous rewards of bicycling through the hinterland of China. The various attractions of package tours, charter flights, Greyhound buses, trailers, car ferries, caravan sites, motels, *pensiones*, youth hostels, bed-and-breakfasts are gauged according to value for money; and, over his toast and coffee, the reader can already blissfully anticipate the great game of Musical Chairs into which the continent of Europe is transformed every July and August.

It would be churlish to object that travelling has thus been debased by the same excessive and premature commercialization as, precisely, Christmas. Nor would one care to align oneself with the splenetic anti-tourism of the literate Right (in such journals as the *Spectator* and *The Times*), with its reactionary nostalgia for a period in which points of arrival no less than means of transport were rigidly classbound: Venice, the French Riviera, the Alps were very definitely first-class; whereas Blackpool, Bognor and the like, and perhaps Boulogne, were steerage. Yet it might be worth examining the parameters of modern travel and their relation to the myth of the voyage.

That there exists a qualitative difference between travel and tourism has long been a commmonplace; and if that difference has an emblem, it is without question the aeroplane. The cramped seating, the flavourless food, one's ever-active fantasies of crashing (the DC10!), the soulless-ness of that hideous antechamber to Heaven, the inter-national (and interchangeable) airport lounge, even one's vague suspicion that the first dozen or so suitcases to trundle on to the luggage conveyor belt are dummies, empty unclaimable placebos − it remains the most execrated of the century's technological marvels. There is, too, the more elevated if equally condemnatory discourse of the 'authentic' traveller: that the aeroplane eradicates space, movement and effort; its kinship, in a cinematic context, is with the zoom (a lens despised by purists) rather than, as is true of a train, with the tracking shot; one disembarks from an aeroplane as from a lift, as though one had not budged at all but had been, in an almost supernatural sense, *transported.*

Which is certainly the case, though not the essential. If the aeroplane has indeed extinguished the exaltation of the voyage, it is because it has made it impossible to 'travel nowhere'. With the aeroplane, the destination is all. Yet, as a verb, 'travelling' is intransitive (or *in transit*-ive): one travels, by rights, for its own sake. Philosophically, this intransitive-ness is supported by the Bergsonian thesis (from *L'Evolution*)

101

créatrice) whereby movement should not be confused with the distance it covers, the latter being in the past, the former in the present, the latter infinitely divisible, the former indivisible. Though the celebrated world-travellers of the nineteenth century were scarcely indifferent to their ultimate objectives (traditionally 'lost': the source of the Nile, the city of Lhasa), these objectives were often part of some larger 'movement' (the Nile in its entirety, Tibet) and their prestige dependent upon the arduousness of the journey as a whole. Thus the fundamental distinction between such pioneering explorers and contemporary tourists lies in the degree to which air travel has dissipated a dialectics of *resistance* (by the jungle, the mountains, the desert) and *penetration* (by the explorer). The aeroplane cannot 'penetrate' (unlike the rocket, whose advent has seen a renaissance of the classic myths and themes of the voyage*) — neither, in consequence, can the tourist.

What does that mean? Consider the following little anecdote, whose very triteness may be the best guarantee of its illustrative capacity. Several years ago, I paid my first visit to Greece and, like the good tourist that I was, decided to go see the Parthenon. Barely hours after my arrival, then, I climb the hill in Athens on which the Acropolis is perched, accompanying fellow-tourists on their way up, intersecting others on their way down. Gradually, over the horizon, familiar to me from scores of postcards, photographs and book illustrations, the Parthenon rises into view. Within minutes, I am standing in front of it. And what I experience is deep disappointment. Why so? Doubtless because of those scores of postcards, etc. Doubtless, too, more subtly, because of an obscure feeling that if I, with all my imperfections, now

*The principal weakness of Philip Kaufman's film on the American space programme, *The Right Stuff*, was that — as distinct from the book by Tom Wolfe from which it was adapted — it never began to convey the sense of space as something to be penetrated. Space, instead, remained essentially (and contradictorily) a *background*.

find myself before the Parthenon — sharing its space, as it were — *then it can't be all it's made out to be*. By, as I fancy, an irrational process of transference, it must be assimilating my imperfections, my inner ordinariness, my secret ignominies.

Yet, beyond this sense of shared, contagious inadequacy, it prompts in me a yearning that I strenuously endeavour to elucidate. I look, I look. I scrutinize the edifice at some considerable length (who knows when next I may return to the spot?). I study its columns from every conceivable angle until I feel I have exhausted the possibilities of purely ocular contact. And I realize that what I desire, somehow, is to *penetrate the Parthenon*, to penetrate the very stones of which it is made up, as one penetrates a jungle or (something I later become aware of when I eventually renounce my sightseeing ambitions and settle for the simpler but probably more authentic satisfaction of lazing beside the Adriatic) as one penetrates the sea. For it would appear to be almost a *conditio sine qua non* of sensual pleasure that it involve or imply a compulsion to penetrate — to be inside (inside the sea, whose cool, ideally even tactility* so inclusively, so *maternally*, embraces one's body that no conventional connotation of 'touching' can do justice to the sensation; inside a bed, its blankets pulled up over one's chin as though in an unconscious parody of swimming; and, of course, inside one's sexual partner) or else taking inside (eating and drinking; or the sexual act for a woman). And it is the tourist's fate, incapable as he is of such penetration, to remain forever excluded from the objects of his languid scrutiny, a eunuch in the harem of the world.

In this, its most recent guise, at least, travel is therefore less 'the art of disappointment', as Stevenson termed it a century ago, than that of *impotence*.

---

*What makes the sea so magical a substance is that it leaves absolutely no spaces between itself and the swimmer, who is 'wet' only when he emerges to the surface.

Derrida Didn't Come

The literary conference — such as one I recently attended at the ICA — constitutes what might be called a *tableau*; or, more accurately, a genre painting, in the purest Dutch manner. For the ideology which that seventeenth-century school of painting belonged to was one of *display*, of, in other words, a frontal, complacently exhibitionist theatricality; and just as, with the complicity of their painters, the good Dutch burghers contrived to transform possession itself — middle-class acquisition — into a spectacle, so these gatherings enable our writers to theatricalize their intellectuality. One can even detect the trace of a 'gestuary', so to speak, proper to the literary conference, of a range and diversity to rival Rembrandt's *The Anatomy Lesson*. Thus one participant lolls on his chair in a posture of unutterable ennui; his nonchalant neighbour doodles in the margin of his sheaf of notes; a third appears to be transfixed by some unseen object offstage, like a centurion in a Renaissance Crucifixion caught dreamily gazing beyond the confines of the frame. The speaker, finally, as though anxious to establish a proper compositional dynamics, has frequent recourse to a single overdetermined sign, the index finger. It is the Word's essential prop; and, just as speaker yields to speaker across the panel, so that oracular index finger — now pointing, now viciously jabbing, now whimsically coiling a stray wisp of hair or beard — also seems to be 'relayed' from one to the other like an athlete's baton.

To complete the tableau, however, and incidentally humanize a scene which runs the risk of becoming too schematic, too 'posed', what is required is a 'humorous and unexpected little incident' or *punctum* (a term from Barthes' *Camera Lucida*). In a Dutch interior, this might be the groping of a maid by a potboy in an obscure nook of the composition or a whippet filching a chain of link sausages from off the kitchen table; and there, at the ICA, as though right on cue, a tapped microphone begins to emit a rude noise, its wire entangles itself around the wearer's shoulder. The writers relax, the audience giggles. It is a cherishable moment, uniting those who speak and those who listen more effectively than any question-and-answer session. Intellectuals are human after all, it reassures us: the helpless prey, as we are, of human accident and error; but also, paradoxically, super-human, for such an incident can only reinforce the tenacious myth of the thinker as, by nature, 'distracted', comically at odds with the modern world.

Yet, like every candid and conspicuous display of owner-ship, whether of material possessions or intellectual intan-gibles, the literary symposium has of late acquired an uneasy conscience. It has been burlesqued in works of fiction by precisely those writers most prone to preside over it (Malcolm Bradbury, in this instance); and if writers, as one ICA panellist sarcastically proposed, are 'the capitalists of meaning', then it may begin to resemble nothing so much as a stockholders' meeting. So what is one to do? The answer could not be simpler: by a characteristically English exercise in slippery self-deflation, one sets about subverting, even negating, one's very motivation for being there.

The main stratagem adopted is one of self-mockery, with those less celebrated for their irony meekly settling for a bewildered air of 'qu'est-ce que je fous dans cette galère?' Thus, in a debate on literary theory as it has currently influenced (or not influenced) English and French writers, and over which it would be reasonable to expect the shadow of structuralism to fall, virtually the only structuralist cited (and at no inconsiderable length) by Bradbury in his introductory speech is the chimerical 'Henri Mensonge', the subject of his own April Fool hoax for a British Sunday newspaper. Thus A. S. Byatt and Jacques Roubaud shrug off theory as externally applicable to the writer's *écriture*, perhaps, but which he or she would be ill-advised to let influence the act of creation. One panellist, a Frenchman, even dares to refer to 'se promenant' — or casually strolling — through the highways and byways of literary history, presumably with pen in hand, though the notion that such an enterprise might imply a degree of labour on his part, of production, is curiously camouflaged. Here, then, is another obscurantist idea, that of the writer as *flâneur*: the fantasy, eagerly subscribed to by frustrated loners on this side of the Channel, of Paris as a literary Utopia, in which one is forever bumping into Deleuze at the Deux-Magots or Genet at the Flore; and the myth of the creative process as, *fundamentally*, keeping company with other kindred spirits.

A second, no doubt more subtle, tactic, employed by numerous panellists, is the persistent deferment of intentions, exemplified by a grammatical tense that I shall name the Future Procrastinate: e.g. 'This morning we shall be discussing . . .' or 'What I shall be attempting to analyse . . .', protestations of an eternally adjourned programme which end by using up the entirety of the speech as delivered. (This tense, it should be added, is more often to be found in the negative: 'Today I shall *not* be looking at . . .', and so forth.)

The third tactic, and undoubtedly the most radical, is that, simply, of non-appearance. It has, I venture to suggest, become so axiomatic of these events for the most prestigious guests to fail to arrive that their absence now qualifies as almost an intrinsic part of the experience. Thus, at the ICA, neither Jacques Derrida nor Nathalie Sarraute, the two stars of the seminar, 'disappointed' our expectations, if one may so phrase it, by making an appearance. Absence as presence, as a structuralist might say? Hardly; and I recall Cocteau's account of the funeral of his friend and fellow-*précieux* Giraudoux. Since the ceremony was pompous and formal, wholly out of character with the witty, mercurial dramatist being interred, Cocteau turned to his companion and sighed, 'Let's leave. Giraudoux didn't come.' Alas! at the ICA, either corporeally or in the sense intended by Cocteau, Derrida didn't come.

A Death in the Family

Fiction has always been something of a snob, it has always *loved a lord*. It has, by tradition, most effortlessly circulated among settings of material well-being; and if novelists have not actually recoiled from detailing the lowlier environment and — by an extension taken for granted until quite recently — lowlier passions of the commonalty, it is nevertheless the case that, with certain eternally cited exceptions (Zola, the Realist School), the proletariat has enjoyed access to great literature only insofar as it could productively contaminate the Olympian, elitist intimacy of the innately 'fictional' classes. Usually unencumbered with any too rigorous socio-political connotations, its signifiers have been, above all, noise, smell and general grossness (meaning 'earthy, uncomplicated life'). To be sure, the situation began to improve in the twentieth century — though, even there, the process of democratizing (one might almost say, desacralizing) the novel was undermined from within by the irreconcilable pre-occupations of the modernist sensibility: apart from Brecht, not one of the great literary modernists ever addressed himself to a truly proletarian theme. Yet wherever the illusionist codes of (popular) nineteenth-century fiction continue to be scrupulously respected — notably, in soap opera — the principle that nothing so immeasurably heightens a personal drama as social prominence (in whatever form of hierarchy) has tended to be reaffirmed.

Consider, for instance, *Dallas* and *Dynasty*, the terrible twins of current television soap opera. Both are what might be called, appropriately enough, dynastic fictions; in other words, a blueprint of the narrative tensions which they generate would be structured exactly on the model of a family tree. But for a family in and of itself to constitute a 'story' (a strategy familiar from many nineteenth-century novels), it must be perceived to be *that* − and not just *any* − family, it must regularly honour and defend its dynastic prerogatives ('Never forget, you are a Ewing', 'We're two of a kind − we're both Carringtons': replace 'Ewing' by 'princess' or 'Carrington' by, let's say, 'Capulet' and the archetypes become evident; soap operas are rhythmically paced by such imperious interjections). Thus, already made aware on a weekly basis of the Ewing or Carrington prestige by the series' preening insistence on an apparently fathomless wardrobe of fabulous gowns and impeccable lounge suits, on sumptuously appointed homes and panelled offices, deep, furry carpets and shivery satin bedsheets, we are also reminded every other minute that the *raison d'être* of these soap operas is a family; that their narrative energy is fuelled by the dramas of kinship with or exclusion from that family; and that the vices they expose (ambition, ruthlessness, egotism) are those which have always attended any overweening emotional investment in family as an aristocratic ideal (i.e. without either a definite or indefinite article).

As for the viewer himself, he belongs (uncomplainingly) among the 'excluded'. Though perhaps married, and also accompanied by an entourage of children, aunts, uncles, grandparents and in-laws, he cannot − certainly not with that hauteur native to the Ewings and the Carringtons − claim 'family'. What his own brood fatally lacks is heredity.

Which is why *Coronation Street* is such an unusual series. Not that its focusing on a street, rather than on a family (or hotel, hospital, office typing pool, etc.) renders it worthy of especial attention. In representational terms, a street may also constitute a closed space, and that of the studio-oriented, interior-bound *Coronation Street* remains in any case a totally implicit, unseen presence, not even vested with the half-hearted 'reality' of downtown Dallas and Denver, recurrent insert shots of whose glossy boulevards punctuate the two American shows discussed above. What *is* unusual, however, is that Coronation Street was devised to impress us as, precisely, *just any street*, a generic space, distinctive by its very lack of distinction. For if the demographic parameters of the series are Northern and working-class, it seeks in no way to vindicate these attributes as ethnic or ideological values. The viewer (that is, the working-class viewer at whom it is unequivocally aimed) is invited to *identify with himself*, so to speak, quite unaided by that carefully computed elevation of social, moral and intellectual standing which has always been deemed (particularly in the cinema) indispensable to the smooth functioning of audience identification (we tend to 'identify' with characters one station above our own). It is almost as though the ambition of the series — again within a working-class framework — were somehow to abolish the screen as a symbol of the closure of the image and the enforced quarantine of its subjects, to grant the viewer, through a kind of audiovisual *trompe l'oeil*, symbiotic access to the cast of characters. And the successful realization of this ambition can best be measured by the periodic applications received by Granada, the production company, from naive viewers anxious to take up residence on the Street should one of its back-to-backs ever fall vacant. (That there does exist such a symbiotic relationship between the characters and the viewers actually seems to be acknowledged by the shot over which the series' credit-titles unfold, row upon row of rooftops bristling with television aerials, as though to foster the illusion that, between 7.30 and 8.00, Mondays and

Wednesdays, the Street itself suspends its serio-comic activities and settles down, like the rest of the country, *to watch the show*.)

The sets represent the zero degree of a designer's craft. The characters are either unglamorous or deglamorized, often downright unattractive by the medium's own standards, and it would be risibly unimaginable for one of them to declare: 'Never forget — you are a Fairclough' or 'We're two of a kind — we're both Barlows' (except in the case of the Street's Mme Verdurin, the would-be *salonnière* of the *Rovers Return*, Annie Walker, whose social pretensions were the butt of gently sarcastic fun). Their humour seldom ventures beyond the sort of 'natural' repartee one overhears at a bus queue or in a pub (e.g. the barmaid Bet Lynch to an unsmiling customer: 'Well, don't laugh — it might crack your face') and their assorted dramas not much more than intensified minutiae, conceivably a trifle *less* exciting than those which the viewer might well be confronted with on his or her own daily round: an inter-city bowling competition, the rearrangement of display shelves in a local mini-super-market, a snatched cuddle in the snooker room of a pub.

One even begins to wonder whether, for devotees of *Coronation Street*, those who would not dream of deserting their posts (*poste*: coincidentally, the French word for a TV set), the peripatetics of 'plot' — its confrontations and revelations — have become a matter of complete indifference; whether what appeals to them is rather a sense of pure continuity, virtually emancipated from the pressure of real incident, from the type of narrative *violence* (which might be represented by unwanted pregnancy or embezzlement, by blackmail or murder) that would risk compromising the show's capacity to mirror the viewer's own existence; whether, finally, their euphoria reaches its height in the mere contemplation (as though from behind lace net curtains) of Bet Lynch cheerfully acquitting

111

her bar-keeping duties or Alf Roberts bustling around his shop. What *Coronation Street* may be offering, paradoxically, is not drama but a blissful relief from drama.

How can it, then, belong to the same genre as its streamlined American counterparts, whose roller-coaster plotlines, like those of some old-fashioned serial, are propelled by dramatic reversals, implausible coincidences and cliff-hanging denouements? What makes *Coronation Street* as well as its equally naturalistic spinoffs, *Brookside* and *EastEnders*, a soap opera? The answer, I suggest, may be found in almost the only attribute that they share with *Dallas* and *Dynasty*: duration. A soap opera is open-ended by definition (which is what differentiates it from such flamboyant Hollywood melodramas, often inaccurately referred to as soap operas, as *Stella Dallas* and *Back Street*). It is, in consequence, essentially a fiction of *survival*. For its own self-preservation, which depends on the viewer being held week after week in seductive, Scheherazadesque thrall, a soap opera is obliged to resort to several devices of suspense and postponement. Not merely the characters but, in a way, the *status quo* is required to survive from episode to episode.

That of the two Ds is maintained by the artless expedient of permitting the industriously scheming J.R. and Alexis to win as many skirmishes as they lose; or, as one commentator wrote of *Dallas* 'by incorporating evil into its sense of order, by making it a crucial factor in the sense of balance and security TV family dramas are designed to provide': a 'sense of balance and security' which therefore allows for the Ewings and the Carringtons, no matter how many internecine plots and counterplots might be in the offing, to sit down each morning at their respective breakfast tables together as though nothing were amiss. *Coronation Street* is also open-ended (hardly news, after a run of almost thirty years). What *it* mimics, however, is the week-in, week-out inconclusiveness of 'life' itself. All the more reason, then, that no crisis should come to disrupt the Street's routine so definitively that it might actually 'close off' the narrative.

Yet there exists just such a crisis, which periodically closes off at least one narrative 'lane': death. Death in a soap opera is, literally, traumatic (as one speaks of a 'traumatic scar'). It temporarily subverts the parameter of duration on which the show is predicated, it disturbs that 'balance and security' already alluded to, it affects the viewer, *toutes proportions gardées*, as it might have affected him were the death to have occurred within his own community of family and friends. And this because, as even the most unsophisticated fan must be aware, it bears a direct, *causal* relation to an offscreen reality.

There are, in effect, three distinct categories to which the death of a soap-opera character may belong. First, where it has been externally imposed on the show by the premature demise of an actor or actress. The most notorious instance of this concerned Jim Davis, the actor who played Jock, the grizzled patriarch of the Ewings in *Dallas*, and whose fatal heart attack caused the plotline of the series to be radically revised. But one might cite several similar deaths among the somewhat jinxed cast of *Coronation Street* (e.g. that of 'Stan Ogden', whose onscreen widow was subsequently compelled by reduced circumstances to put her house on the market); and, more recently, the French series *Châteauvallon*, that nation's 'answer to' *Dallas*, was brought to an abrupt conclusion by a car accident in which its leading lady was seriously injured. Second, where it has been internally imposed, often without the accord of the performer himself, who is then forced to leave the series trailing clouds of publicly aired resentment. A 'controversial' example of forced dismissal was that of Noele Gordon, the star of *Crossroads*, whose betrayal was somehow compounded, in the popular mentality, by the actress's own death from cancer a year or so later. Its *reductio ad absurdum* was attained in the episode of *Dynasty* which ended with practically the entire cast being gunned down by terrorists: apparently, only those performers prepared to sign the production company's new contracts were allowed to survive the carnage. Third, where it has been necessitated by a performer's resolution not to renew his contract (usually through fear of typecasting). Bobby Ewing (Patrick Duffy) was murdered, Fallon Carrington (Pamela Sue Martin) perished in an aeroplane crash (only to be 'reincarnated' by another actress), and so on. In a special case, Len Fairclough, one of the pillars of *Coronation Street*, met a brusque demise when the producers of the series judged that the actor Peter Adamson, after having been prosecuted for gross indecency (a charge of which he was, as it happens, acquitted), was no longer decently identifiable with the character he played.

Here, in a way, is the ultimate in illusionism. A character's condition is equated with that of the actor playing him,* his death is vindicated, 'paid for', by the sacrifice of his *alter ego* (and the lesser fate of dismissal can only be viewed, in these Thatcherite eighties, as a *little death*). Yet there could be considered something salutary, as well, in the notion of the television viewer, conditioned to treat death either as a statistic (the news) or as a rhetoric *(Starsky and Hutch, Miami Vice*, etc.), being confronted with a genre in which — at least, from time to time — it has a meaning, a *sting*.

---

*The shooting of J.R., the climax to one series of *Dallas*, was actually alluded to in the BBC news bulletin which immediately succeeded it.

Culture and Nature

Every traveller has experienced the sensation (one which succeeds at the same time in orienting *and* disorienting him) of the scenic characteristics associated with a given country (the disposition of its fields and meadows, the incidence of mountains, torrents and gorges) abruptly vanishing at its frontier and being instantly supplanted by those of the country he is about to enter. From countless examples one might cite the thoroughness with which an archetypical 'French' landscape appears to have translated itself into 'Italian' by the time one resurfaces from the Simplon Tunnel; or the feeling, for anyone crossing the United States by car or Greyhound coach, that (again from a purely scenic point of view) each of its states is, in reality, as different from its neighbours as is its miniaturized equivalent on a multi-coloured map. But the most vivid demonstration of all is that received by the traveller returning to Britain from the Continent. Notwithstanding the stereotyped urbanization of the International Style, with its ubiquitous freeways, flyovers and high-rise blocks of flats, one is immediately conscious of being *home*, in England — no longer in 'Europe'. Yet since the green and even-tenored vistas of the English Home Counties are practically identical to those of Northern France, it is, of course, not Nature itself* that prompts such a feeling but the way in which it has been (agri-)culturally appropriated,

*I have capitalized Nature and Culture wherever they represent pure concepts.

115

colonized, by the respective nations: a colonization expressed in the presence or not of hedgerows, the shape and size of farmhouses and churches, the nationally distinctive punctuation of road signs (which are, in England, less sleek and streamlined, less neutrally 'internationalist' than in France), the incongruity over here of red phone booths and postboxes, and indeed this country's prevalent tendency towards primary, almost toy-bright hues.

I used the word 'incongruous' to describe the juxtaposition of a red phone booth and the countryside in which it has been deposited. It is, however, seldom perceived as such. And one might even go so far as to suggest not only that phone booths (and postboxes, road signs and level crossings) have become so integral and humanizing a part of what is meant by rural Britain that it is their absence, rather, that would strike us as incongruous; but also that, their textures coexisting as harmoniously as they do, they bear out a basic truth concerning man's relationship to his environment: which is that in time Nature becomes Culture and Culture becomes (a second) Nature.

How, to begin with, does Nature become Culture? Through art, evidently, the most 'noble' repository and conductor of a culture. For us, nature has long since ceased to represent (if it ever did) innocent matter. It has been irreversibly sublimated by painters, poets and musicians, to the point where it has become possible to inscribe landscape, like architecture, within a history of styles (Romantic, neo-Classical, Expressionist, etc.). It has, in a sense, been made 'stately', as one speaks of a 'stately home'*: city-dwelling children, for instance, are dispatched on excursions to the country as though to an art gallery. In other words, Nature is regarded as a value sufficient unto itself, and one not

---

*By contrast, when travelling abroad, what one tends to look for in nature is a picturesque alienness or what might be called an 'untamedness'.

unrelated to an ideology of class. The modern environmental conservation crusade, notably at that ecolo-pastoral end of it which habitually applies itself to the defence and reclamation of 'green belts' and the restoration of cottages and tiny provincial railway stations, remains essentially middle-class in origin and support; and there are times, these days, when one is tempted to believe that Nature is 'natural' only insofar as the existence of a middle class might itself be considered a natural phenomenon. As for the industrial classes, they have doubtless felt less motivated by the mania for conservation: quite understandably, since a passion for conserving nature is frequently contingent upon what one already possesses of it. Without the likelihood of ever purchasing a weekend cottage in Norfolk or reconverting the stables on the estate of a manor house in the Cotswolds, the instinct (entirely laudable in itself) to protect and enhance its natural environs − its 'view', in short − must appear less of an urgency than a luxury.

Nature, then, has not only been cultivated but culturized: it has upheld rather than broken down sociocultural in-equalities, just as its produce (food, clothing) continues to do; and, ignorant of all but the most basic biological forms and functions, the layman (for nature, too, divides us into laymen and experts) increasingly exploits it as a vast, anthropo-morphic *machine à métaphores*, as an image bank. No specialized acquaintance with the oak or willow as living, growing organisms is required for anyone to recognize that the former connotes manly vigour, the latter a sort of melancholic languor; if a valley cannot be described as 'fertile', then it is a poor thing, as is a mountain not 'snow-capped' or a moor not 'lonely' (and haunted, whatever its geographical situation, by the ghosts of Cathy, Heathcliff and a legion of escaped convicts).

It might be replied that literally nothing on earth is secure

117

from man's incorrigibly metaphorizing disposition, his propensity to invest every feature of his environment with both a meaning and a morality. But take, precisely, a postbox. In one of Chesterton's Father Brown stories, titled 'The Invisible Man', the scene of the crime (a murder) is a nondescript suburban villa in which the victim lived alone and to which, or so testified a number of irrefutable witnesses, no one was admitted. Since a crime indeed occurred, however, that 'no one' was necessarily someone *disguised as no one*; and, it transpires, the murderer disguised himself as the postman, the 'invisible man', to whom next to no attention was paid as his presence at the villa was routine, insignificant — in a word, 'natural'. If one does not seek it out with the intention of posting a letter, a postbox, too, is invisible; likewise, a telephone booth, a Belisha beacon, a set of traffic lights, a zebra crossing, etc. Either as autonomous structures or as the components of a complex grid of culturally determined signs and stimuli (the city), these impinge on our daily urban consciousness as pure functions, rarely as forms. Unless we happen to be particularly attentive to the history of industrial design, we do not stop to admire them. How, in any case, would one judge the aesthetic validity of a red postbox, the gentle parabola of its beret-shaped dome, the precise width of its oblong slot, the way its colour harmonizes (or not) with all those other colours in that vast supermarket of signifiers that the city has become for us? On what criteria? Even in the countryside, as I have suggested, it will end by being seamlessly — one might say, organically — absorbed into its environment. In fact, it no longer partakes of Culture but of (a sort of) Nature. It has 'put down roots'. It has been endowed with the 'immortality' of a tree. It may not be noticed, but it is obscurely *loved*. (Significantly, there has evolved out of the Pop-oriented tradition of modern English art a 'suburban pastoral' mode for whose practitioners red postboxes and the like constitute the ultimate, nostalgic traces of an idealized and cosily claustral Britishness: the movement's guiding spirit is Peter Blake.)

It is normal, then, for contemporary urban man, both physically and spiritually alienated from his roots (as everyone believes), and from the soil in which these roots are immemorially implanted, to develop as rich and intimate a contact with the paved or macadamized crust of urban geology, as well as with the orchard of signs, of a Marvellian luxuriance, which germinate from it. And since Nature, even in this figurative, mineral sense, will *always* end by being recuperated by Culture, it ought not to surprise us that insensitive urban planning is invariably surrounded by controversy: e.g. proposals to alter the design of street lighting, to streamline London's taxis and buses, to withdraw pound notes in favour of coins; one might mention, too, the much-publicized distaste of tenement occupants for the 'soulless' high-rise flats in which they are to be rehoused. Redesigning a telephone booth is no doubt an act of less 'tragic' import than axing a centuries-old oak tree; yet it is also, in its way, a form of institutionalized vandalism.

The Fellow-Travellers' Club

The commercial – and, one must suppose, also critical – success of Julian Mitchell's play *Another Country* was doubtless founded on the way it definitively interpenetrated two of England's most enduring sociocultural myths: the public school as an exotic microcosm ('I sensed I had an idea about all this that no one else had had,' the dramatist hopefully mused in an interview. 'The point about public schools is that they are microcosms of the larger world outside'); and (as one might call it) the 'intelligentry' as double agents in the class struggle. It did not, in other words, do much more than confirm a strange national prejudice that Marxism is, *essentially*, something that goes on at the choicer English public schools, like cricket and buggery, and that the great majority of Marxists, when not barrel-thumbed and bloody-minded trade unionist bolshies, have been patrician class traitors, usually of homosexual inclination, weaned away from their hereditary privileges by an illusion of economic egalitarianism specific to the thirties. Though, taking the word in its wider application, 'history' has never been one of this country's best subjects, it is dispiriting nevertheless to see what is by far the most influential political philosophy of the twentieth century (arguably its *sole* philosophy) so reduced to the cavortings of a few frivolous adherents. For if, as English eccentrics and mountebanks, Burgess and Maclean, Blunt and Philby may just be regarded as worthy of Waughian satire, they simply cannot support the ideological weight which Mitchell (and, by its complicity, his audience) has brought to bear upon them.

Though *Another Country* is, in itself, an amply mystificatory work, it acquires its full significance only when assimilated into a cycle — including, notably, Alan Bennett's drama *The Old Country* and his much-lauded television film *An Englishman Abroad* — a cycle of which the end is probably nowhere in sight. Each of these plays defines Marxism as, by its very nature (and by a reversal, too, of current geopolitical realities), a form of *dissidence*; as somehow anchored in 'eternal' opposition to an idealized vision of English society and its (no less 'eternal') values; and as being incapable of integration into that society without the despoiling of its traditions and textures. The opposition, moreover, as is clear from the three titles cited, is a primarily *geographical* one. In the first pair, the crucial noun 'country' is ambiguously confronted with, rather than qualified by, 'another' and 'old'; in the third, the polarity of 'Englishman' and 'abroad' could scarcely be more explicit. But then, geography has always supplied one of the great latent justifications of crude anti-Communism, and it is quite conceivable that the fortunes of Marxism would be very different today had its primal Revolution taken place, not in an inclement Russian October, but during high summer, let's say, in Rome. It is almost as though, for the knee-jerk anti-Communist, the concepts of *Marxism* and *snow* have become inseparable, as though two kinds of climate, political and meteorological, have henceforth been rendered indivisible,* as though the barometric horror of the USSR's geographical location might be appropriated as a handily God-given metaphor for the soul-numbing monolithicism of its bureaucratic apparatus. And

---

*There do exist, to be sure, Marxist regimes in more tropical (and topical) climes — Cuba, black Africa — but these tend to be perceived as 'grafted on' and therefore interim.

there is nothing more calculated to set that elemental deep-freeze in vivid relief than to have it juxtaposed with the finest that England can offer in the way of breezy, unbuttoned, old-school-tie nonchalance – in short, the best type of British spy.

Thus, in *An Englishman Abroad*, the viewer's perception of the Soviet Union is filtered through the down-at-heel but still jaunty charm and elegantly scurrilous theatrics of an ageing Guy Burgess; and virtually the only argument proposed by the film in response to a doctrine whose complexities have engaged a good number of the century's foremost thinkers is: 'Communism is *dull*!' Embodying a somewhat different but just as potent Englishness is the character played by Alec Guinness in *The Old Country*, a forlorn defector who languishes in his up-country dacha in a wistful haze of Elgar and Vaughan Williams, the King's College Choir and those Metropolitan place names (e.g. Peckham Rye, Islington Green, Camden Town) whose nostalgic exploitation has become Bennett's stock-in-trade. As for the protagonist of *Another Country*, based also on Burgess, it would be a perverse spectator indeed who did not prefer his youthful, shamelessly elitist self (played by foppish Rupert Everett as little more than a Modiglianiesque homosexual pin-up, what with his artfully tousled hair, his shirt-tail protruding from his grey flannel trousers and his deliciously smelly socks curling round his ankles) to the sad, embittered and politically lobotomized loser shown, three decades later (and in the film version only), being interviewed in a dingy Moscow apartment. In each case, an exceptional, 'larger-than-life' being – what is more, one who personifies the kind of personal disorder, the behavioural extroversion, which, as we are regularly informed, is constitutionally frowned upon by the Soviet authorities – finds himself set up in opposition to a callous, tentacular officialdom; and, as anyone at all

conversant with the codes and conventions of popular fiction
(e.g. *The Scarlet Pimpernel*) might easily predict, the
spectator's sympathies are guaranteed in advance.

Three related mythologies, then, can be seen in interaction
with each other: the myth of Communism as a 'climatic'
phenomenon, a fundamentally alien system proper to, and by
rights containable within, the uncouth, inhospitable hinterland of Northeastern Europe (whereas a Westerner's
wanderlust almost invariably lures him South); the myth of
theoretical Marxism as an aberration indissolubly linked to
the theme of espionage and quite unthinkable as a dogma that
any sane Briton would unconditionally, and under no
coercion and for no monetary advantage to himself, subscribe
to; and that, finally, of Marxist practice as − once again by
definition − foredoomed to disillusion and failure, with each
of the plays focusing, none too coincidentally, on its hapless
hero at a moment of disenchanted self-realization.* (Though,
to be fair to it, *Another Country* does attempt to convey
something of the intellectual fervour which must once have
accompanied such a dramatic conversion to the Communist
cause, the gesture is irretrievably trivialized by the fact that
Mitchell has attributed Burgess's politicization to his ire at
being ostracized from the so-called 'Gods', a hyper-exclusive
public school society!)

One is amused to note, by the way, how both dramatists
use 'images' of England and Russia so that each can be

*That, within a populist framework, another approach is feasible was demonstrated
by Warren Beatty's flawed but moving film *Reds* (a commercial flop, admittedly). In
Reds, the October Revolution was presented (with no less hindsight than by Bennett
and Mitchell) as a *dream*, sullied and irredeemably compromised, perhaps, but still
pregnant with meaning and truth. Unlike so much of the American cinema,
founded on the illusion that blasting a man's face off with a Magnum revolver by
day will make one a better lover by night, Beatty's romantic melodrama proposed
(naively, but so what?) that it is because one has endeavoured to 'change the world'
that one becomes 'good in bed'. (Even the snow in *Reds* was of a downy,
Christmassy weightlessness.)

invested, complementarily, with the piquancy in which, taken separately, it might prove most deficient. Communism isn't exactly a theme to entice coach parties up Shaftesbury Avenue? Then 'civilize' it with lashings of Eton, Elgar and espionage. The public school ethos has been complacently pawed over once too often? Then confront its incestuously inbred self-fascination with the great currents of history. Each, in this manner, will act as the alibi and antidote of its opposite.

There is yet another myth, however, which has been mixed into the batter, a more insidious one whose application far exceeds the importance and influence of the three plays in which it may be exposed. Even if both *The Old Country* and *An Englishman Abroad* are set in the present day (as is the prologue to the film of *Another Country*), they have all been injected with the distilled essence of a much earlier decade: the thirties, of course. I have already mentioned the average Briton's chronic incapacity to conceptualize history and situate himself within its flux of meaning. Yet what Mitchell and Bennett are disingenuously exploiting is an excessive *selectivity* of historical consciousness. The effect of their plays is to confine, however prematurely, the constructive or 'creative' phase of Communism more or less to a single decade, to neutralize its potential contemporaneity (the eternal refrain of Marxism as a 'spent force') and render it, along with various other quaint *isms* – Fabianism, d'Annunzism, Poujadism, etc. – evocatively 'period', even kitschy. But to immure an idea thus in the past is to deny it not merely a future but a present – a *presence*. The same process can be seen at work with the word 'fascist'. That has, it is true, degenerated into a facile, catch-all insult, employed with a scary lack of discrimination. *Yet a word may also be corrupted by those who decline to use it*; and to insist on identifying 'fascism', in the name of some dubious semantic pedantry, exclusively with its historical, upper-case F manifestation in Italy, Germany and Spain, or else to apply the adjective so sparingly that it covers only those individuals, factions and systems of government 'to the right of Genghis Khan', as a current jibe has it, is (consciously or not) to blind oneself to the fact that it flourishes still, and will presumably continue to flourish, wherever and whenever personal liberties are chipped away in the assumed interest of the collective (and notably, alas, in the Communist bloc).

So much, to be sure, that once seemed clangorously urgent has since been consigned to the 'dustbins of history' (beginning with that dated locution itself, I suppose). Mao Tse-tung, for instance, is routinely perceived as, at best, this century's Confucius (with all that that implies in 'Oriental', i.e. gnomic and unproductive, rumination), his Little Red Book has value only as a slim relic of sixtiesiana and the fractured faithful of moist Maoists (if any, indeed, survived the débâcle) have become as redundant, in historical terms, as the superannuated hippies still to be sighted peddling sandalware in Nepalese bazaars. In their diverse contemporary transmutations, however, and for better or worse, Marxism and fascism are *not* moribund — on the world stage, if not on those of the West End. And it is surely time for the English intelligentsia to enter (or re-enter) the debate as real travellers in history rather than as the clubby fellow-travellers too many of them apparently flatter themselves to be.

Page 3

It is a happy accident that the British tabloid press opted for such glinting, elemental epithets as *Sun*, *Star* and *Mirror* for, as may be confirmed by a glance at their interchangeable pages, they reflect more than they inform. Or rather, they inform by reflecting, in all naivete, like so many Messieurs Jourdains of semiology, a remarkable number of the themes, myths and structures through which our society defines itself.

A fine specimen of this reflective power is the famous Page 3. As everyone knows, it has become a tradition, in these newspapers, for one page to be sacrificed to a usually full-length photograph of a feminine nude or semi-nude. There is a reasonable diversity in the poses adopted (though, if one were to monitor their progress more closely than I have been able to do, one would in all likelihood find the same or similar ones recurring with the mathematical regularity of numbers on a roulette wheel, the 'pool' of such odalisque postures being a severely limited one), as there is in the types of personality (now languid, now pouting, now peek-a-boo, now 'healthy', i.e. rural and, by an infallible extension, busty). And if one is soon made aware of a profound uniformity of effect, this derives less from a certain technical negligence (these are not pin-ups in the literal sense, it being difficult to imagine someone actually pinning up a page from the *Mirror*) than from an almost total absence of what might be called erotic 'punch'. It is the latter factor which I wish to consider here.

Predictably, the vast majority of these photographs exploit

a basic trope of (soft-core) nudity. The model seeks to conceal what are pleasantly termed her erogenous zones and, by her doing so, the erotic charge is displaced on to the act of concealment itself. Though an occasional set-up will make a half-hearted gesture in the direction of a more elaborate pose − one model listlessly sprawls across a fluffy white fur rug (fur being still a negotiable sign of feminine lasciviousness); another, of the 'healthy' genus, sits half-naked on a milk-maid's stool, tugging at a cow's udder as gingerly as a dandy drawing off a yellow kid glove − most of them appear perfectly content to remain totally standardized. This is mass-produced nudity, the nudity of neither-nor: the model is neither plump not skinny, neither salacious nor demure, neither accessible nor inaccessible; and, as we shall see, neither fully clothed nor fully naked. A fundamentally anti-erotic nudity, then, since eroticism − for which dispositions of setting, costume (invariably 'scanty') and physical 'type' are primordial − requires at the very least that choices be made, decisions taken, in the matter of presentation. The Page 3 'lovely' is intended, in the brief moment before the page itself is turned, to be *one thing to all men* (more accurately, to all the male readers of whichever newspaper she happens to be appearing in). She is not, on the other hand, meant to be the object of any individual's masturbatory fantasy. Hers is the transparent nudity of the beach (and the increase of nudity in the popular press has described an exact parallel to that found on 'family' beaches): disturbing when first encountered, but rendered well nigh invisible by repetition.

Yet here, as distinct from on a nudist beach, one does detect an element of titillation, contingent upon the fact that, though I have referred to them as nude, these models are always slightly less than naked. Breasts are routinely bared, buttocks fairly often: the genitals, by contrast, are never exposed, their concealment being effected by a small bikini

127

bottom or, if the model is completely naked, by the self-conscious coquetry of her pose. The titillation, however, is not due to any belief on the reader's part that her ultimate sanctum will eventually be infringed: he has learned to interpret the code too well to entertain such an illusion. It arises rather from his certitude that her nudity must remain forever in suspension, like the three dots which end without ending a sentence left deliberately 'open'. For it is in the very nature of voyeuristic eroticism that it can be reduced to an affair of *punctuation*. The erogenous zones demand not only to be seen but to be *read*; and, to be read, they have to be punctuated. Thus a nipple defines a breast by 'punctuating' it, and he who has not been allowed to see the nipple has not (quite) seen the breast. Thus, too, the buttocks are 'punctuated' by their cleft. As a result, even if the flimsy swimsuit modelled by a young woman for a colour supplement spread encircles her bare buttocks in a loop as narrow as the cleft itself, she is not 'naked'. Nor is the dancer in some old-fashioned revue whose nipples are masked by two glittery, star-shaped badges. The codified trio of erogenous zones — breasts, buttocks and genitals — may be compared to the winning arrangement of fruit on a fruit machine: a state of true nakedness is arrived at only when all three 'come up' simultaneously. Which means — reverting to our original metaphor — that what would effectively complete, what would definitively close off, the complex or (in the case of a tabloid newspaper) simple sentence that is a woman's body in representation is not, paradoxically, the three suspension points of a tiny, triangular, sheath-like *cache-sexe* but the full stop of her genitalia.

3-2-1

Sociologists, socio-anthropologists, structuralists, students of the media, and even moralists — practically everyone will find something to mull over in the popularity of the television quiz show. For just as in the natural world phenomena exist whose metaphorical allusiveness has contrived to precede and obscure, in our perception of them, their basic 'thereness' as expressions of beauty or sources of knowledge — the type of insect, for instance, which buzzes a few millimetres above the surface of a pond and on sight of which no one can fail to be instantly reminded of a speedboat — so the wealth of 'meanings' produced by almost any quiz show makes it near-impossible for an 'intellectual' of whatever discipline (I mean merely, anyone prone to reflecting on what he sees and hears) to watch it 'in the first degree', without irony and strictly for relaxation.

To begin with, the situations that are structurally analogous to the quiz show — those, at least, that come most easily to mind — are seldom 'positive', which is already a fact of some interest. Whether one thinks of Pavlov's experiments or the common practice of training animals by rewarding every advance with a biscuit or a lump of sugar; of a school examination or a nuclear countdown (the latter analogy clearly conveyed in the name of one such programme, *3−2−1*); of a police interrogation or a courtroom cross-examination (emphasized by the sensationalist *mise en scène* of *Mastermind*: black leather armchair, ominous lead-in music, the solitary pool of light in which the contestant is bathed), the suspense generated by quiz shows is founded essentially on public humiliation.

And it becomes all too obvious that intelligence is the least of their concerns. What *Mastermind* is designed to test, of course, is neither intelligence nor even knowledge but memory — memory as a purely numerical, accumulative function (recalling the most dated, most discredited forms of schoolmastering), one naively binary in structure, each question being 'reciprocated', as though within a closed circuit, by its single correct answer. More intriguingly, one cannot help but notice that the competitors in several of the lighter shows possess astonishingly few of the qualifications one might have expected. Their command of 'general knowledge' strikes one as, if anything, lower than the average. Confronted by a garrulous presenter with a silvery, sparkly microphone brushing his lips as nonchalantly as a cigarette, they grace the television sound stage not as experts in any given field but as attractively sheepish specimens of 'ordinary' (i.e. lower middle-class) humanity, surrounded, as it were, by their own tiny patch of natural habitat like stuffed seagulls or otters in a provincial museum.

The fact is that participants in TV quiz shows are (or rather, become) *stereotypes* hardly less than the characters of the soap operas and situation comedies bookending them at peak viewing hours. Thus, in an episode of one quite overwhelmingly populist show, *Mr and Mrs*, which questions married partners on each other's ritual habits, fads and (a favourite word of its presenter) 'quirks', an elderly competitor was asked whether her husband was likely to know the name of the then current Foreign Secretary. There followed a moment or two of reflection, before she replied that he wasn't. Whereupon, the husband himself stepped forward to be directly quizzed on the said politician's identity: a commensurate racking of brains produced the simple answer, 'I don't know'. And this admission of ignorance was greeted by a burst of applause from the studio and the presenter's breezy '*Ab*-solutely correct!' Which is, if unintentionally, a gag. Yet, aside from the fact that nothing could better reveal the very relative breadth of knowledge required of a competitor, this comic *reductio ad absurdum* demonstrates the speed with which such 'non-professionals' are assimilated into the medium's extended family of drolly stereotypical Britons (as witness, too, the title *Mr and Mrs*, which sounds more like that of a weekly domestic comedy series; the show's insatiable appetite for humorous, often mildly salacious, details of its participants' lives, to which the studio audience responds with gales of laughter; and so on). To appear on television, whatever one's status, is to *perform* – from that there is no escape.

But the high-water mark of any quiz show (as their presenters themselves repeatedly claim), and to which the question-and-answer session is little more than a prologue, is the revelation and distribution of prizes. This is the moment the studio audience, and presumably that at home, has been waiting for – to paraphrase the prescribed formula. And these days, as it happens, participants in quiz shows tend to be rewarded in kind, with consumer goods (furniture, cars, elaborate video cameras and camping equipment), more often than in cash. Why so? In part, no doubt, because television is a predominantly visual medium, one for which, as also in the cinema, money acquires a value only if it can be de-abstracted or 'visualized' – only if, in short, as in a heist movie, one can actually see what a million dollars *look like* (tight wads of banknotes snugly tucked inside a metal suitcase). Quite obviously, such visualization is unthinkable on a quiz show. On the other hand, there is something mean, insubstantial and unspectacular about a cheque (which is why cheques photographed in the hands of newspaper bingo prizewinners are invariably larger-than-life). Prizes, after all, have an obligation to be conspicuous; and the apparition of a dining-room suite or a mobile cocktail bar (invested with the dull — one might say, *matte* — kitsch typical of most furniture on display), dramatically unveiled from behind a curtain by some glamorous feminine assistant, ends by transforming the show's presenter into a sort of professional magician.

There is also, I believe, a moral rationale behind the selection of such prizes. Charity and corruption — and the liberality of the quiz show partakes a little of both — acquire an easier conscience when the medium of their exchange is non-monetary. (To a tramp one prefers to offer a sandwich rather than money, which one suspects he will immediately spend on alcohol; doubtless a public official suffers less guilt if bribed with the keys of a new sports car than with a bulgy envelope surreptitiously slipped into his pocket.) And it is finally a very particular kind of charity which one thinks of when watching a quiz show: that still practised by the Salvation Army. What matters above all for the habitués of Salvation Army hostels is, first, hot food and drink, then (fairly) clean bedding. Yet, in order to *earn* these comforts, they too are required to perform, or so we are told: namely, to sing hymns and be lectured at. It may well be, then, that the strictly 'quiz' element of a quiz show — which is, as we have seen, undistinguished by too much ostentation of intellect — is nothing but an updated and glamorized version of that (generally recalcitrant) hymn-singing by which the destitute pay for their nightly sustenance and rest.

E.T. and the Poets

How is one to define anti-poetry? Let us simplify grossly: anything that resembles, without actually being, poetry. Grossly, but not unjustly: for it is resemblance — in its most familiar literary mode, that of metaphorical analogy — which for a slovenly reader constitutes a near-infallible sign of the poetic. It is by measuring his thralldom to the imp of analogy that the public is wont to recognize the poet's 'touch' — in prose as well as in verse. And whenever (certainly, in the recent twentieth century) a poet has contrived to enjoy unaccustomed public favour, one takes it as almost a given that his poetry is little more than a vehicle for the manipulation of such analogies; that his readers are prepared to tolerate some possibly rebarbative verse forms for the sake of a cluster of ingenious metaphors; that these metaphors should clearly and even clamorously affirm their presence in the text (the metaphorical conjugation has to strike the reader as instantly legible); and that, further, like so many poetic one-liners, they should be just as quantifiable as the gags in a Neil Simon comedy, i.e. the more of them there are, the better the poem.

Of late, the question has ceased to be an academic one. Poets (a few poets) have been barnstorming around the country by helicopter, and their collections sell in the thousands. Now that is, on the face of it, a good thing for poetry — except that one is tempted to enquire, which poetry? And, there, the myth becomes all the more flagrant

133

for being so wilfully assumed: the poetry of the Metaphor. I refer to the 'Martian' school, so named because its self-appointed objective is for the reader to confront his natural environment with the inconographical innocence of an alien, a Martian, an E.T. As one approving critic wrote of the movement's pacesetter, Craig Raine, 'He has set himself the mammoth task of visual retrieval, forcing us to see for the first time things we have been looking at all our lives.'

Were this really the case, it would not be a novelty. 'Making strange', observing the commonplace from an uncommon angle so that it might be reinvested with a poetic lustre, is at least as old as modernism itself. But, as it happens, it is not the case. In fact, the very epithet 'Martian' (though specifically italicized by Raine in the title of his best-known collection, *A Martian Sends a Postcard Home* – with its unfortunate yet irresistible echo of 'E.T., Phone Home') proves something of a misnomer. When, in his poem 'A Free Translation', Raine writes of 'the pagoda of dirty dinner plates', for instance, he could hardly be less Martian, since, for an authentic Martian (supposing such a creature existed), a pile of dinner plates would be just as obscure and just as exotic as a pagoda. Instead of 'making strange', then, one might describe his project as one of 'making familiar', the pagoda (a 'poetic' image in English) being de-exoticized by its superficial resemblance to something as humdrum as after-dinner crockery. And the predominant feature of Raine's work is this conscious tendency to make familiar, to *domesticate*, any artefact which would otherwise risk disconcerting the reader. Thus from another poem, 'The Widower':

> . . . jelly fish
> like wilted Dali watches . . .

('Wilted' is redundant, surely. And it is Dali, not Raine, who has made the world strange — by arbitrarily jellifying the texture of watches. What Raine does, on the contrary, is correct the painter's Surrealist intuition by reverting to the jelly fish that may well have been in Dali's mind in the first place.)

From 'Circus':

> . . . no usherette
> by Salvador Dali
> with a drawer in her midriff
>
> full of ice cream . . .

(Again he borrows a Dalinian invention [or convention]; and again he manages to defuse the metaphorical charge. For, like a twisted spring disentangling itself with a metallic shudder, what the poem really evokes is the sense of oneself perusing one of those warped feminine forms peculiar to Dali and quipping, fairly wittily, 'Isn't she like a cinema usherette?' As for 'full of ice cream', it would appear to suggest that Raine is unconfident of the legibility of his comparison and panic-stricken at the idea that the reader might have to ponder it for a moment, might have to raise his eyes, even fleetingly, from the page.)

As one can see, the characteristic trait of Raine's meta-phors (similes, rather) is, paradoxically, their pedantic, fundamentally tautological literalness. 'This looks like that' is what they say, over and over again; and so, in most instances, it does; and that, it would seem, is that. Except that, on occasion, in a startlingly maladroit fashion, he will even go so far as to metaphorize their ostensibly neutral connective tissue. Thus, from 'Rich' (the title poem of his most recent collection):

> . . . and these are her eggshells
> cracked on the kitchen table
> like an umpire's snail
> of cricketers' caps . . .

(The basic simile is garbled by that snail creeping in, quite superfluously, between the eggshells and the umpire's caps.)

This may appear as mere quibbling; and so it would be were it not for the fact that Raine's work, along with its public success, exposes a certain mythical notion of what verse is or ought to be. The metaphorizing impulse − here sorely abused − is, of course, a constituent ingredient of much of what we recognize as poetry. In the work of any major poet, though, it takes its proper place within a plurality of rhetorical figures and practices, not the least of which is a bright, hard, crystalline literality. What gives Raine's verse, by contrast, a debilitating lifelessness and lack of resonance is precisely his Thesaurus-like cataloguing of objects and their 'synonyms'. In poetry (which Barthes designated the Utopia of language), a word almost never coincides with its own definition, but represents the spot − one might say, the *headland* − from which that definition starts to become visible. If a word were ever allowed to reverberate in Raine's poems, however, it would fatally compromise the analogy which is often its sole *raison d'être*. Thus, on the page, the strange, un-pregnant flatness of 'coolie hats' in these lines from 'A Free Translation':

> In coolie hats,
> the peasant dustbins
> hoard their scraps . . .

Or, from the same poem, the way in which Hokusai's most celebrated print is dispossessed of all its agile sensuousness:

It is time to eat
the rack of pork
which curves and sizzles

like a permanent wave
by Hokusai . . .

Still, if the language of Raine's poetry remains obstinately unresonant, there is something vibrating *between* that language and the reader — something, moreover, which enables us to situate not only the source but the significance of its appeal. Consider a few examples not-so-randomly extracted from *Rich*.

From 'In Modern Dress' (a cod Elizabethan parody of childhood):

Sir Walter Raleigh
trails his comforter
about the muddy garden,

a full-length Hilliard
in miniature hose
and padded pants.

How rakishly upturned
his fine moustache
of oxtail soup . . .

From 'Code Napoleon':

. . . and one child, executing
his angry flamenco . . .

From 'The Widower':

. . . saluting the sun
out of our eyes . . .

From 'Circus':

> My daughter tells me
> she has seen a man
>
> behind a trailer
> with seven tangerines
> he shares out equally
>
> between both hands . . .

That last example delivers the telltale phrase — 'My daughter tells me . . .' It is assuredly not an accident that the presence of childhood is so strong in these poems. What is the 'child', after all, in mythic terms, but a sublimely unconscious, a gloriously unprofessional, manifestation of that tenacious bourgeois ideal, the genius? What, then, in the same terms, is the 'poet' but a grown-up who has somehow preserved intact, miraculously uncorrupted, a primeval child-like vision? And what, finally, are the poems of Craig Raine if not the latest, most blatant and unashamed avatar of poetry as a higher species of the cute solecisms uttered by 'innocent' children? Contemplating a dustbin lid, the child likens it to a coolie hat; watching a man shield his eyes from the sun, he or she naively asks whether it might be a form of salute; and the attendant parents, aunts and uncles will dotingly coo, as sure as night follows day, 'Don't children say the funniest things!' Such is Martian poetry.

The Incisive Fossa

Physical beauty — what is commonly intended by that term — appears to hold no great interest for intellectuals. For a century now (in this country, perhaps ever since Walter Pater) there has been nothing remotely resembling an aesthetics of physical beauty; nor is its significance *defended* (in the sense that one defends a university thesis) by any of the current theoretical disciplines: the debate has simply ceased to be. Behind this conspiracy of silence may be detected, first, a socio-ideological rationale. The prestige of physical beauty — as, at least, a subject for discussion — has no doubt been eroded by our increased alertness to every kind of racist, sexist and elitist abuse. Even those questions which would serve as one's point of departure — What is physical beauty? How is it organized? — already seem to be presupposing the objective, measurable existence of something which may, in reality, function only as a projection of our fantasies. They presuppose, too, that (if it exists) it is by nature indivisible and hierarchical; that there are not, in short, as many variations on physical beauty as there are physical or racial types. So that *any* reflection on the subject might be claimed to represent yet another instance of the Occident (the word by which Western Europe and the North American continent are designated in the codified languages of fascism and crypto-fascism) insidiously asserting its 'natural' supremacy.

But there is also a *moral* interdiction. Such beauty, for the moralist, constitutes not only an irrelevant but a highly dubious quantity, in that it — equally so, its absence — risks obscuring the authentic, profound, i.e. *inner*, nature of an individual (his or her 'soul', 'heart', 'character', however one chooses to name it). Though this particular argument is all but exhausted by the lapidary banality of a proverb ('Beauty is only skin-deep'), it does continue to sustain a good many bourgeois myths attached to human relationships. Not only bourgeois ones, apparently: from the otherwise fairly complete (and alphabetically arranged) roll-call of amorous figures making up Barthes' *Fragments d'un discours amoureux* (*A Lover's Discourse*), one is a trifle surprised by the omission of any rubric based on the letter B — indeed, of any significant allusion to the relevance and implications of physical beauty.

What is, however, most problematic for theoreticians is that physical beauty depends less on the internal organization of facial features than on their *coincidence*: one's basic reaction to a perfectly realized face-object, as to any coincidence, is: *I don't believe it*. Though physical beauty (like similar manifestations of beauty) is a paradoxically abstract property, it cannot be mapped. Though, on an exquisitely beautiful face, the eyes, the nose, the cheekbones etc., impress us as scarcely less absolute than a set of geometrical figures, it is difficult to conceive of a Euclid of the physiognomy. And though, as was said, it possesses a genealogy of idealized (and racist) archetypes, physical beauty nevertheless remains too elusive, too morphologically ambiguous, to be reduced to the diagrammatic singularity of an Identikit image.

Yet who would deny the importance it assumes in our lives, its capacity to *haunt* us? In which light I myself am prepared to admit to a (no doubt) perverse predilection for a kind of magazine to whose targeted readership I totally fail to conform. Or rather, to two related kinds of magazine: either those populist film fan reviews whose 'copy' — little more than gossipy snippets of information — serves mostly as an alibi for extensive photo-spreads of personable young actors and actresses, not stars, as a rule, but 'up-and-coming hopefuls'; or else what are called 'fanzines', identical in style to the former except that even less attempt is made to conceal the fact that their primary attraction is the sex appeal of a cluster of current film and pop idols.

An example of the latter is *16*, an American monthly whose cast of characters (virtually unchanged from issue to issue) is made up of such youthful film and TV performers as Matt Dillon, Ralph Macchio, C. Thomas Howell, Diane Lane (all of whom received their sultry apotheosis in Francis Ford Coppola's *The Outsiders*), the child actor Ricky Schroeder, Darryl Hannah (best known as the mermaid in *Splash!*), and the pop singers Duran Duran, Michael Jackson, Madonna and so on. (That the majority of names cited happen to be masculine is due to *16*'s popularity among teenage and prepubescent girls. But there is, in any case, something particularly poignant about physical beauty in a male adolescent, where those traits usually regarded as 'feminine' – delicacy, fragility, gentleness of expression – are thrown into relief in a way that is not possible with a young girl, in whom they have been completely normalized.)

It would be naive to imagine such beauty as somehow innocent of ideology. Even aside from its occasionally callous capitulation to market forces (whenever a member of the teenybopper pop quintet Menudo, for instance, reaches the crucial, almost cabalistic, age of sixteen, he is *contractually* required to resign from the group in order that new blood may be injected into it – a ritual sacrifice no less ritually described by *16* as 'the end of an era'), there is hardly a page in the magazine which does not offer clear evidence of a *vision*: that of a nostalgic, tacitly Reaganite, America of surfboards, sneakers and steady dating, personified at each end of its inhibitively narrow ethnic spectrum by Schroeder's

Teutonico-Californian blondness and Macchio's dark, fawn-eyed Italianicity (though now apparently in his early twenties, Macchio has handily retained the physical immaturity of an adolescent).

Yet the faces remain. Exploited as they are, their charm (as also their vacuity) is that they have not yet been invested with the onerous sub-text of 'character'. Nothing can be extrapolated from them, nothing can be read into them, they express nothing except the endearingly vacant spectacle of their own youth and beauty. Thus it becomes possible to take pleasure in a face, to *savour* it, without the individual's interiority eclipsing, so to speak, its purely formal parameters: a face whose eyes are merely eyes, not 'the windows of the soul', whose chin — *still fresh*, as one says of paint — cannot easily be interpreted as either weak or pugnacious. I exaggerate, of course (though it may be by exaggerating that one arrives at a semblance of truth): the stigmata of experience, however rudimentary, or of an evolving consciousness, however uncultivated, are already perfectly legible on all but the most immature faces. Which is why one might situate the focal point of such youthful allure, its 'centre of gravity', in a facial feature whose very anonymity has rendered it impervious to the advancing encroachment of significance, of personality: I mean the moist little furrow which separates the nose from the flowing, monogrammatic M of the upper lip and which is called the *incisive fossa*.

The incisive fossa conveys nothing beyond a vague sense of the flesh's buttery malleability (I recall, as a child, being told that it represented 'God's thumbprint'). It serves no discernible purpose and responds to no formalized erotic impulse. Though, from face to face, it presumably varies in shape and size, it has never been so classified. And though accorded prominence in a handful of mildly homophiliac films of the fifties — notably, *Rebel Without a Cause* with

James Dean and Sal Mineo, *Splendour in the Grass* with Warren Beatty, and *West Side Story* with Richard Beymer (along whose 70mm fossa I longed to run barefoot!) — even there, it tended to be upstaged by the smoky chiaroscuro of the nostrils, the tiny, satiny highlight of the lower lip and the liquid softness of the eyes. Unlike these features, however, unlike practically every other part of the face or body, the incisive fossa has never been burdened with anthropomorphic pathos (e.g. straight, 'powerful' shoulders connoting moral rectitude; a thick, red neck connoting brutish insensitivity and philistinism; long, tapering fingers connoting the artistic temperament). It is, in short, and self-contradictorily, what I should like to call the *anonymous signature* of facial beauty.

Le Booker Nouveau Est Arrivé

Though the mind gorges itself on all kinds of delicious pastries – opera, ballet, cinema, and so forth – the Book remains its loaf of bread. For that is what a book is, mythically speaking: a (home-baked) loaf of bread, the staple of the intelligence. And what – for the majority – most decisively betokens an individual's mental superiority is his readiness, his strange lack of reluctance, to 'stay home with a good book'. (The question, in literary terms, of just how distinguished that book should happen to be is an irrelevance: it is in the book itself, in its *essence* as a book, that the goodness is perceived to reside.) A problem with books, however, is that, for a period in which whatever is not (audiovisually) representable all but forfeits its right to exist, they remain private, almost hermetic objects. Even when held open, they are, by their very nature, *closed*. Reading is also 'the beast with two backs' (or spines), the reader open to his book, the book open to its reader, in a mutual intimacy as exclusive and inaccessible as that of two lovers. How does one 'represent' a book, after all? As a mere cultural artefact? Yet it is so much more than that. In adapted form? Yet not all books are (as this word may be applied to an unusually resourceful person) 'adaptable'. Few, in any case, survive being distilled to their plotlines alone. And what becomes of language, the generative fuel of our relationship with any book of literary value?

The problem is quite a serious one, since books are no less subject to the laws of supply and demand than any other commodity, and our shopping (or window-shopping) habits are increasingly conditioned by the media − by television in particular. But whereas a film-maker may succeed in rendering a book 'whole', in its materiality as well as its spirituality (Godard, for instance, in certain of his early features), television's failure in this domain has until recently been total. There were, in truth, no real book programmes on television, only 'author' programmes. Which should not surprise us, given the basic incompatibility of the book and the box − the snag was that the author, if he proved to be a TV 'natural', often ended by obscuring his own work. The odd exception apart (*The South Bank Show*, *Arena*), a book would be judged of interest because its author seemed so, not vice versa; and a so-called 'in depth' profile of a writer (a fairly rare occurrence, in any case) began to resemble a book with, say, 250 pages detailing its author's *curriculum vitae*, his opinions on women, politics, God, Chinese cuisine, etc., and an easily missable rear cover flap on which might be read a compressed summary of the novel (or whatever) in question. And, as the results were, to say the least, inconclusive (the principal argument submitted for the failure of such programmes actually to promote books being that TV addicts have never been among nature's more voracious readers), it must have been felt, by publishers and programme planners alike, that a more vigorous approach would have to be adopted.

The solution was the Booker Prize. The Booker Prize existed, to be sure, before it was infiltrated, in the mid-seventies, first by the press, then by television, just as the continent of America existed before it was discovered by Columbus. But it attained its quintessence, as both a function and a spectacle, only when, with the obliging connivance of the media, half the nation's (literate) population started to find its attention irresistibly drawn to the collective cerebration of a panel of writers, critics and scholars whose names, for most of them, vaguely 'rang a bell', if that. Since then, not only are Booker prizewinners assured of a multifold increase in the number of copies sold, but the titles remaining on the shortlist (and, it is claimed, books in general) benefit proportionally from the attendant publicity.

Analogies have been drawn with cinematic, political or sporting events. Yet, despite all the painstakingly cultivated suspense – that of an Oscar ceremony in the first, BBC-produced broadcast (presided over, hilariously, by Simon Winchester and Selina Scott), that of a minor but crucial by-election in ITV's subsequent coverage (presided over by Melvyn Bragg) – these are not the most appropriate. Since it was essential for the success of the Booker Prize that the world of books as a whole be implicated in its prestige, it became necessary, paradoxically, almost to underplay the importance of individual novels and their authors and concentrate instead on the *year*: in other words, to invest books with the concept of *vintage* (an idea cribbed, aptly enough, from the French: the Booker might reasonably be regarded as the British Goncourt). For if a book is the intellect's loaf of bread, why should it not also be its wine, that inevitable 'poetic' complement to bread? The rest is, as they say, history; and now, every October, during the run-up to the prizegiving itself, the classic connoisseurial anxieties can be heard expressed: Is it a good year? A disappointing year? A vintage year?

The operation (for that is what it is) has described an exact parallel, from its modest initiation to its triumphant outcome, to that designed to stimulate awareness of the arrival of *le Beaujolais nouveau*. It is by being trained to view the production of books, as of wine, as a cyclical, annually renewable process (the respective harvests are reaped in the same months each year) that the public is made – for a month or two, at least — as book-conscious as it is wine-conscious. No matter its past inexperience in either domain, it is accorded easy, rapid and painless access to taste and discernment. Everyone, in short, becomes a connoisseur — for a day.

Is there cause for complaint? Wine and literature are both, after all, potentially beneficial 'substances', and neither should be the exclusive province of an elite. Even so, it might be worth pointing out that the immense, and immensely successful, campaign in favour of Beaujolais is precisely that: *a campaign in favour of Beaujolais*. Beaujolais is not in any literal sense a brand name, I know, but it nevertheless represents a single commercial interest. There exist many other excellent French wines — and many, too, from elsewhere in the world. There likewise exist many excellent books which are not at all of the Booker *cru*.

This Is Your Life

Let me first propose, *gratis*, and for the attention of any author of whodunits in urgent want of a plot, the narrative schema of an as yet unwritten thriller. It belongs to the classic English tradition, except that, instead of in a snowbound country vicarage or else aboard a mysteriously stalled coach of the Orient Express, the shortlisted suspects would be interrogated inside a television studio; and, instead of from the hyperactively devious cogitation of Hercule Poirot's 'little grey cells', it would be from Eamonn Andrews, and whatever skeletons are rattling between the blood-red covers of his *This Is Your Life* album, that they might guiltily be tempted to shrink.

The situation is one rich in suspense and dramatic potential. Andrews confronts the evening's subject in his customary fashion, steering him on to the stage before a hushed and expectant studio audience. He opens the album and prepares to narrate its contents, when a gunshot is fired from the wings, fatally wounding his guest — the victim, manifestly, has harboured some dreadful, festering secret with regard to one of the visitors from his past. That secret lurks, most plausibly, somewhere within the biographical data of Andrews' album (unless, of course, there should happen to be nothing at all within its pages, a hypothesis I have entertained more than once); and it is through such usefully compiled and annotated information, as well as by questioning each suspect in the prescribed manner (a ghastly parody of the show's own format), that the Great Detective (invited by happenstance to attend the performance in the company of his friend, confidant and 'Watson') will ultimately succeed in identifying both the motive and the murderer. (The sole flaw, as I see it, of this excellent scenario is that, in compliance with the conventions of traditional whodunits, the murderer ought properly to be, as we know, the least likely suspect − in other words, Eamonn Andrews himself!)

My schema, fanciful as it may appear, is nevertheless founded on a concrete reality: the structure of *This Is Your Life* is quite patently that of a *trial*. Consider: the victim (as he is in effect designated), while going about his business, is accosted by Eamonn Andrews with the brusque aplomb of a police inspector; and even if he is not advised that anything he says will be taken down and may be used in evidence against him, the unanswerable authority with which Andrews actually pronounces the preordained phrase: 'Mr − , this is your life!' renders its implications comparably ominous. (Escape, in any event, is apparently out of the question and has been attempted on remarkably few occasions.) The 'defendant' is then ushered into a public courtroom where Andrews − his role henceforth becoming a specifically judiciary one − proceeds to call the first witness. The court is in session.

It is when one asks oneself what the charge might be that one begins to recognize the show's peculiar (though, on television, perfectly routine) bias: for, if *This Is Your Life* resembles a trial, it is, miraculously, a trial *without prosecution*. Witness follows witness (all of them what a court of law would term 'character witnesses') to testify to the defendant's charm, wit, talent and generosity, and above all his essential *authenticity*, his inveterate horror of pretence and affectation, his unfailing good humour in adversity. So many ladders, so few snakes! And even those snakes which − in the early years of his ascension, particularly − he could not avoid

149

encountering (failures, reversals, temporary setbacks) are retroactively transformed, by the show's hagiographical approach, into ladders; or rather, into Stations of the Cross which have to be traversed by every aspirant on the path to televisual canonization. The charge is therefore not fame in itself (precisely the justification for the defendant's appearance on the programme in the first place) but the negative attributes popularly imputed to fame or success: egocentricity, ruthlessness and conceit. And, as one might well predict, not one of these maudlin trials has ever ended in anything but acquittal, with the tearily grateful subject surrounded, embraced, by those who have helped to exonerate him.

This Is Your Life is itself of only very marginal interest, a programme for which a powerful sense of (unintentional) humour is required, certainly if it is to be watched all the way through. It constitutes, however, one of those rites of passage to which every 'personality', every darling of the media, will sooner or later be called upon to expose himself (others which might be cited are the various TV chat shows; on radio, *Desert Island Discs*; and such regular 'quality' newspaper columns as 'A Room of My Own', 'A Life in the Day', etc.). And, in each case, by a clammy complicity between the interviewee, the interviewer and, it is to be feared, the viewing public, the former emerges unscathed, even exalted.

Evidently, nothing of what I have just written will come as a surprise; and the 'average viewer' — who, I rather suspect, tends much of the time to gaze at his television *set*, so to speak, rather than at any individual programme — appears reasonably content with the indiscriminate hum of enthusiasm that it emits like articulate static. (As, to their chagrin, producers and advertisers are starting to realize, television has become of late a kind of audiovisual *radio*, secreting an uninterrupted ooze of information to which no more than flickering attention need be paid.) It is, all the same, possible to express astonishment at just this refusal to be astonished, at the universal assumption that it is in the very nature of the medium to fawn over those to whom it regularly gives audience. One would not insist, to be sure, that the guests of a chat show be exactly 'grilled': only that — like any, as they say, self-respecting newspaper or magazine — the show admit to the possibility that they might have characterial shortcomings; adopt a critical attitude towards their achievements ('critical' not necessarily in a pejorative sense); retain a degree of scepticism when confronted with their publicly proclaimed motivations; and, in short, treat them as (gifted, prominent, even unique) human beings, not as saints to be offered up to the camera-God. As it is, whenever a TV interviewer endeavours intermittently (or Walter-Mittently?) to sound a trifle more abrasive, he is soon recuperated by the piously conformist discourse of his elected medium.

Nothing is more calculated to 'show its age' than television. Nothing is more likely to strike our descendants in the decades to come as quaintly 'period' than the toadying sycophancy and Steinway smirks of an Eamonn Andrews, a Russell Harty and a Bob Monkhouse. And if, as I have suggested, *This Is Your Life* takes its structure from a trial, it is finally, in reverse (and in a minor key), of the great show trials of the Stanlinist 'purge' that one is most forcefully reminded. Like justice, a life after all is easily travestied.

Under the Sign of Cancer

Cancer, a myth, a mythology? Indubitably: it is, in fact, one of the most potent and perennial of our *fin de siècle* (or *millénium*). We are currently haunted by twin phantasmagorias, one internal, the other external: death by cancer and nuclear annihilation, or the Big C and the Big A or H, their iconographies neatly overlapping in the coincidence of form between a malignant tumour and a nuclear cloud (the mushroom thus becomes the great cryptic motif of the eighties).

Indeed, cancer is honeycombed with all sorts of meanings. There is, for instance, the frequent exploitation of the disease as a metaphor of political disgrace or psychic repression (John Dean warning President Nixon that 'there is a cancer eating at the White House' or Norman Mailer justifying having stabbed his wife by the claim that, had he not done so, the sublimation of his impulse would have engendered a cancer): in her study, *Illness as Metaphor*, Susan Sontag brilliantly analysed the way in which this discourse has pervaded orthodox thinking. Then, on a more literal level, and by a mechanism illustrated earlier in my essay on paedophilia, it responds to our yearning, in an age of insecurity, for some ultimate, immutable measure.* We 'need' cancer because, by the very fact of its incurability, it makes all other diseases,

*The purest expression of this mechanism is the near-ritual invocation of Hitler's name in conversation. E.g., if an individual one distrusts is defended as charming, one has only to reply, 'Hitler was charming, too.'

152

however virulent, *not cancer*. ('At least,' one may hear it said, 'it isn't cancer!')

However, the discreet fatalism with which the disease has come to inform our lives is beginning to foster a less terrorized, more Stoic, more serenely defeatist response. All roads lead to cancer: or such, increasingly, is the impression we gain from television documentaries, magazine articles and specialized books. There would seem to be no escaping its occult and tentacular influence. From X-rays to hair-driers, from maraschino cherries to processed peas, from sunbathing to *not* sunbathing, artefacts and activities we previously felt authorized to take for granted are now — it is impressed upon us, more or less urgently — *hazards*. Yet, so generalized has the threat become, it is paradoxically the hazard itself which has been rendered tolerable, taken for granted. And I think of one of Kafka's parables, in which a religious ceremony is so regularly interrupted by the intrusion of a leopard into the temple, come there to drink the wine from its chalices, that the high priests end by anticipating its intrusion and integrating it into their sacrament. What, then, is cancer if not our leopard? We do not so much die of it as live with it; more exactly, we live with the foreknowledge that we will eventually die of it. We have made it part of the sacrament of our worldly existence. And, in its universality, in what strikes us as its quasi-ineluctability, it has become almost a synonym for Death itself. As such, it affords us a certain peace of mind.

Memories

1. I remember a little boy in Italy who fell into a well, never to be recovered alive. I remember, too, that London's *Evening Standard* published a headline prematurely announcing his rescue and was obliged to retract it in the following issue.

2. I remember travelling on Clyde steamers to the island of Arran and a once popular resort named Rothesay.

3. I remember that the poster for *How to Marry a Millionaire* depicted the film's trio of leading actresses (Marilyn Monroe, Betty Grable and Lauren Bacall) vivaciously striding towards us, arm in arm.

4. I remember Mick Jagger spending a night in a prison cell (for a drug offence, perhaps?) and 'writing a poem' about his ordeal.

5. I remember Drobny winning the Wimbledon championship; and how, as children, playing lawn tennis in the street, we all wanted to 'be' Drobny.

6. I remember when there seemed never to be a period without a new dance craze.

7. I remember a board game, Totopoly, so-called because it was set in a horse-racing milieu. However, it proved not to be

satisfactory, since there were two quite separate ways in which one could win: by riding, or merely by betting on, the winning horse. As I recall, my friends and I played it only a couple of times before reverting to Monopoly and Cluedo.

8. I remember Dr Barbara Moore walking from John O'Groats to Land's End and back again; and a second (male) long-distance hiker to whom she referred contemptuously as 'that Johnny-come-lately'.

9. I remember that on the original LP sleeve of *My Fair Lady* a benign Bernard Shaw, ensconced in Heaven, dangled Rex Harrison and Julie Andrews on puppet strings. I also remember a fad for cashmere cardigans *à la* Professor Higgins.

10. I remember tasting Coca-Cola for the very first time. It was at Prestwick Airport (or 'Aerodrome', as it was then known) and was offered me by an American serviceman.

11. I remember Spinola, the Portuguese 'Kerensky', with his monocle, his flamboyantly braided uniform and his resemblance to a decadent aristocrat in a Simenon novel.

12. I remember the craze for matching shirts and ties, usually of a flower pattern.

13. I remember that Sophia Loren served a two-week prison sentence for tax evasion.

14. I remember, as a teenager, quite regularly shoplifting sweets from Woolworths.

15. I remember wearing a roll-neck, 'angry young man'

pullover, so long and stringy it almost reached my knees.

16. I remember blue- and sepia-tinted photographs in early issues of the *Illustrated London News*, which I used to leaf through in my childhood.

17. I remember hoops-and-sticks.

18. I remember myxomatosis.

19. I remember the advertising slogan, as famous as it was (apparently) ineffectual: 'You're never alone with a Strand', as well as the jingle:

> You'll look a little lovelier each day
> With fabulous Pink Camay.

20. I remember Piper Laurie.

21. I remember, from TV comedy shows, the ubiquitous qualifier 'diabolical' (as in 'a diabolical liberty'); and, for the mouth and nose, 'cakehole', 'bracket' and 'hooter' (as in 'one up the hooter').

22. I remember that the first time I saw the word 'rabbi' in print I thought it was a typographical error for 'rabbit'.

23. I remember, in the early fifties, purchasing with a ration card a quarter-pound bag of broken biscuits.

24. I remember Van Cliburn.

25. I remember Harry von Zell, eternally discombobulated by Gracie Allen's solecisms in *The Burns and Allen Show*.

26. I remember when *The Times*'s front page consisted exclusively of personal columns.

27. I remember *The Adventures of Hiram Holliday*.

28. I remember that the two imposters of English history were named Perkin Warbeck and Lambert Simnel.

29. I remember Classic Comics; and, as it happens, those which I remember most vividly were adaptations of novels which I have not since encountered between hard covers, e.g. *Under Two Flags*, *Two Years Before the Mast* and *Pitcairn Islands* (the sequel to *Mutiny on the Bounty*).

30. I remember, as a child, enthusiastically recommending the film *Botany Bay*, starring Alan Ladd and James Mason, to my grandmother and her elderly friend, who (to my mortification) loathed it.

31. I remember that Albert Finney 'disappeared' into the Amazonian rain forest for two months or so.

32. I remember Queen Mary's boxy toque hats and multi-stringed pearl chokers.

33. I remember bubble cars.

34. I remember a walking race whose leading participant was in a pitiable condition as he neared the winning tape, his eyes glazing over, his tongue hanging out, his knees buckling under him. (And, if I am not mistaken, he was eventually beaten.)

35. I remember modelling, out of silver paper, what I imagined Blackpool Illuminations to be.

36. I remember a Tex Ritter speaking record which I believe was called 'The Old Violin'. In any event, it concerned a battered old violin up for auction and receiving paltry bids of a dollar, two dollars, etc. Whereupon, from the depths of the auction room, a grizzled, weatherbeaten hobo steps forward, picks up the instrument and begins, hauntingly, to play it. The bidding then rises by thousands of dollars; and, when asked to explain its sudden increase in value, the auctioneer replies in a tone of wonderment that the old violin has been ennobled by 'the touch of a master's hand'. There followed a little homily applying the fable to life itself and whose details I have forgotten.

37. I remember Sir Francis Chichester and Sir Alec Rose.

38. I remember when, in the fifties, the Japanese were accused of systematically counterfeiting Western products and, in particular, whisky (there apparently existed a Japanese 'Johnnie Walker', for instance).

39. I remember a fad for making lampstands out of Chianti bottles.

40. I remember being eight-and-a-half years old.

41. I remember listening to Adamov's play *Ping-Pong* on the Third Programme.

42. I remember the American situation comedy series *I Married Joan*, with Joan Davis, Jim Backus (who, as I knew, also dubbed the voice of Mr Magoo) and another actress, Beverly something, who played their ungainly next-door neighbour.

161

43. I remember writing to a pen pal in Tasmania with the formulary address of house number, street, city and country expanded to take in *Europe, The Western Hemisphere, The World, The Solar System* and *The Universe.*

44. I remember the fashion for pyjama parties, come-as-you-are parties (concerning which everyone appeared to have heard of a friend receiving his or her invitation while in the bath) and cheese-and-wine parties.

45. I remember satire.

46. I remember reading Graham Greene's *Our Man in Havana* and being inspired by the example of its protagonist to start a collection of miniature liqueur bottles. I never owned more than half-a-dozen (they turned out to be more expensive than I had expected) and I have no idea what eventually became of them.

47. I remember 'Oh, the Esso sign means happy motoring . . .' and the cartoon commercial which it accompanied.

48. I remember the yodelling of Frank Ifield.

49. I remember never feeling cold as a child and being puzzled, even in midwinter, by the complaints of grown-ups.

50. I remember an American satellite disintegrating in space and causing everyone to wonder, a trifle apprehensively, just where it would re-enter the earth's atmosphere. It landed, if I remember aright, partly in Australia and partly in the Pacific.

51. I remember how erotically aroused I was by the poster for *Cat on a Hot Tin Roof*, on which Elizabeth Taylor, wearing

only her slip, lounged suggestively in front of a huge brass bedstead.

52. I remember the cover of a Penguin edition of *The Catcher in the Rye*: at its centre, where one might reasonably expect a portrait of the author, J. D. Salinger, there was nothing but a blank space.

53. I remember being taken to see Disney's *Snow White and the Seven Dwarfs*. What frightened me was not the witch nor the chase through the forest but the outwardly unscary scene in which the dwarfs, marching downhill to their little cottage, sang 'Hi-ho, hi-ho, it's home from work we go' and the 'Hi-ho' refrain progressively diminished in volume until they had disappeared from view.

54. I remember when Maurice Chevalier (whom I had heard of but never seen) was a regular guest on a Saturday night television show, *Café Continental*, hosted by a Frenchwoman named Hélène Cordet.

55. I remember Lord, and especially Lady, Docker.

56. I remember Patrick Campbell's stutter on *That Was The Week That Was* (often abridged to TWTWTW or TW3).

57. I remember when scampi represented an ideal of the good life.

58. I remember the red-and-green spectacles one wore in order to watch a 3-D film.

59. I remember the first, often-repeated commercials on Channel 4: one, in particular, for a brand of videocassette

tapes featuring the Pink Panther; another for dog food, in which a breeder would assert, more accurately than he knew, 'I've said it before and I'll say it again . . .'

60. I remember farthings, threepenny bits and George V (and even Edward VII) pennies.

61. I remember Spike Milligan ad-libbing nightly during the run of *Oblomov*.

62. I remember trigonometry.

63. I remember when it took almost a minute for a television image to materialize on the (eight- or twelve-inch) screen after the set had been switched on.

64. I remember a joke about two men who are crossing the Sahara and one night hear a voice enumerating: '1, 2, 3, 4, 5 . . .', etc. They are both utterly mystified as to its origin until one of them chances to read on the spine of his packet of Player's cigarettes: 'It's the Tobacco that Counts.'

65. I remember the first time I heard Marianne Moore's definition of poetry: 'An imaginary garden with real toads in it'; and the first time I saw Saul Steinberg's satirically diagrammatic cartoon of New York City.

66. I remember the trumpeter Eddie Calvert and his hit number 'Oh, My Papa'.

67. I remember, every winter, making 'slides' (a pastime which appears not to interest children today).

68. I remember, not all that long ago, a monstrous traffic jam

stretching halfway across the continent of Europe (it had been provoked by striking lorry-drivers).

69. I remember television interludes: a potter's wheel, a tankful of tropical fish and an accelerated, four-minute train journey from London to Brighton.

70. I remember reading *Nineteen Eighty-four* when the year itself seemed to belong to some dim and unknowable future.

71. I remember Donald Campbell breaking the speed records on both land and sea.

72. I remember, on *Tonight*, the late Kenneth Allsop's shirts (invariably striped), his hair (too long at the neck) and his missing leg.

73. I remember 'Slow, slow, quick, quick, slow'.

74. I remember that Connie Francis was raped in an American hotel room.

75. I remember confusing Ray Ellington, who supplied the musical numbers on *The Goon Show*, with Duke Ellington.

76. I remember Rachman and Rachmanism.

77. I remember that the Gambols' first names are George and Gaye. (But how do I know this? For I never read the *Sunday Express*.)

78. I remember Alan Hackney, author of the books on which were based the films *Private's Progress and I'm All Right, Jack* (though the latter novel was, in fact, titled *Private Life*).

79. I remember the Moorish symbol from the Villa Mauresque found on hardback editions of Somerset Maugham.

80. I remember Tony Hancock's TV address: 23 Railway Cuttings, East Cheam.

81. I remember that, at a time when his facial features were not widely known in this country, Walt Disney was a guest on the 'celebrity spot' of *What's My Line?* On his entering the studio, the audience scarcely reacted; once he had 'signed in', however, there arose a tremendous burst of applause. I also remember, from the same panel game, that the masks worn by the male panellists were modest black dominos, whereas those of the women were elaborately 'feminine' and frilly.

82. I remember when people wore a lapel badge depicting a horrible little grinning face.

83. I remember, as a child, taking my trousers and underpants down in a forest to find out what it felt like.

84. I remember Charlie Kunz, Winifred Atwell and Russ Conway.

85. I remember hearing, at various times of my life, the reputedly authentic story of a lorry transporting strips of corrugated iron, one of which slips off behind and decapitates a motorcyclist. Yet, because of the speed at which the motorcycle is travelling, it continues to keep pace with the lorry, whose driver, paralysed by the sight of a headless rider, collides with another vehicle and is himself killed.

86. And that reminds me that Jayne Mansfield was also

decapitated in an automobile accident. But I have no idea what subsequently became of her husband — and, physically, her exact male equivalent — Mickey Hargitay.

87. I remember a deodorant advertisement whose slogan began 'Someone isn't using . . .'

88. I remember, when Krushchev visited the set of *Can-Can* in Hollywood, how offended he was by the scantiness of the dancers' costumes.

89. I remember the first time I employed the phrase 'Twenty years ago . . .' in relation to my own adult life.

90. I remember the studio audience shouting 'Open the box!' on the quiz show *Take Your Pick*.

91. I remember that the actor Christopher Beeny, who played one of the kitchen staff in *Upstairs, Downstairs*, had also been Lenny Grove in *The Grove Family*.

92. I remember Armand and Michaela Denis.

93. I remember the maracas of Edmundo Ros.

94. I remember a humorous definition of an intellectual: anyone who, on hearing the *William Tell* Overture, is not automatically reminded of *The Lone Ranger*.

95. I remember Michael Foot's dog Dizzy.

96. I remember when there existed rival British airline companies, BOAC and BEA.

97. I remember the fad for what were called 'mind bogglers', e.g. 'General de Gaulle clipping his toenails', 'the Pope gargling'.

98. I remember the *couturiers* André Courrèges and Paco Rabanne.

99. I remember the Beat poet Lawrence Ferlinghetti.

100. I remember snake-clasp belts.

101. I remember that it took an unconscionable time for the ailing Franco to die; and that Tito's death throes were similarly protracted.

102. I remember the catch-phrase 'See you later, alligator', to which one was supposed to reply, 'In a while, crocodile'.

103. I remember receiving a hundred lines from a Latin master for having giggled at the word 'homo' (which, of course, means 'man') and discovering very much later that the etymological root of 'homosexual' was not the Latin 'homo' but a Greek word meaning 'the same' (as in 'homonym' and 'homogenous').

104. I remember the Vassal affair (and I once glimpsed John Vassal himself, a few months after his release from prison, catching a train at Victoria Station).

105. I remember the conjuror Channing Pollock.

106. I remember a hippie in Trafalgar Square advising me to 'do my own thing', the first time I had encountered the expression.

107. I remember magnets (in their traditional horse-shoe form, red with twin black tips).

108. I remember John Paul Getty III's severed ear.

109. I remember the television cooks Fanny and Johnny Craddock; and, earlier, Philip Harben.

110. I remember believing in Santa Claus, but I have no memory of the precise circumstances in which I ceased to believe in him.

111. I remember, and I still possess, the first pocket calculating-machine I ever bought. It seemed, at the time, quite miraculously slim, though in comparison with what is currently to be found on the market it now strikes me as lumpy and graceless.

112. I remember that John Dean had a svelte blonde wife named Mo, and John Mitchell a rather tragically eccentric wife named Martha.

113. I remember Op Art.

114. I remember Sherpa Tensing.

115. I remember that the French novelist Céline died on the same day that Hemingway shot himself.

116. I remember the craze on American campuses for squeezing as many people as possible into telephone booths.

117. I remember, in my childhood, having a weakness for uncooked jelly.

118. I remember the excruciatingly deliberate manner in which Ian MacDonald, a Ministry of Information spokesman, would announce the latest news from the Falklands.

119. I remember the blond Swedish boxer Ingemar Johansson.

120. I remember unravelling golf balls.

121. I remember hand jiving.

122. I remember that the third, and least publicized, of the Gabor sisters was named Magda.

123. I remember that one used to hear quite regularly of young couples eloping to Gretna Green.

124. I remember the sixties fashion for suits of a cod-Regency cut (with enormous flapping lapels, for instance).

125. I remember inspecting a friend's collection of un-franked Andorran stamps and wondering whether anyone had ever actually received a letter from Andorra.

126. I remember the colour of Cary Grant's socks in the celebrated 'crop-dusting' sequence of *North by Northwest*: sky-blue.

127. I remember how I used to enjoy sliding the two hemispheres of a small terrestrial globe (attached to a sickle-shaped stand) back and forth along the Equator and inspecting the various permutations in which the world's land masses would be realigned.

128. I remember that the Edinburgh Festival's logo (a miniaturized reproduction of which appeared in the *Radio Times* whenever the BBC relayed one of its concerts) used to be Cocteau's Orpheus profile with lyre.

129. I remember another logo, that of the Festival of Britain: a weathervane motif surmounted by a helmeted Britannia.

130. I remember when one stood to attention for the National Anthem at the end of the last evening performance of a film.

131. I remember Lotte Reiniger's shadow films.

132. I remember newsreel footage of Soviet tanks in the streets of Budapest and Prague.

133. I remember Elsa Maxwell.

134. I remember when British Rail was known as British Railways.

135. I remember the death of Sibelius.

136. I remember two of the Goons' nonsense songs:

> Ying tong
> Ying tong
> Ying tong
> Ying tong
> Ying tong iddle-i-po

and:

> I'm walking backwards for Christmas
> Across the Irish Sea.

137. I remember the bizarrely curdled appearance of the Red Sea when 'divided' by Moses (or Charlton Heston) in Cecil B. De Mille's *The Ten Commandments*.

138. I remember meeting a little boy who had never seen the sea.

139. I remember, in Hollywood films of the fifties, how obsessed the feminine characters were with mink coats.

140. I remember how delighted I was to find an ice cream cone in which the ice cream had been packed right to the tip of the cone.

141. I remember Johnny Ray's hearing aid and the manner in which he crooned: one hand would grip the microphone, while the palm of the other cupped his good ear.

142. I remember Sara Keays and Sarah Tisdall, though I am already beginning to confuse them.

143. I remember the 'topical' calypsos of Cy Grant.

144. I remember concrete poetry.

145. I remember that, on *Panorama*, the French 'child-poet' Minou Drouet, suspected of not being the true progenitor of her verse, was locked alone in a room for the duration of the programme and requested to produce a poem. Which she did.

146. I remember the four-minute milers Roger Bannister and Chris Chataway.

147. I remember the joke:
'Why is Croydon called Croydon?'
'Because it's near Croydon Airport.'

148. I remember, in *Lacombe Lucien*, the pungent Southern accent of Pierre Blaise when, asked whether he was pleased with his new plus-fours, he replied, 'Pas telle-ment'. I also remember that Blaise bought a motorcycle with his fee from the film and was killed soon after when it crashed.

149. I remember the Queen of Tonga.

150. I remember Sgt-major Brittain.

151. I remember the Yeti.

152. I remember never being able to locate a nosh bar recommended as serving the best salt beef sandwiches in London.

153. I remember when almost every nation in the world seemed to be governed by a 'Grand Old Man': Churchill in Britain, Eisenhower in the United States, Adenauer in West Germany, Nehru in India, etc., and I cannot help wondering what has happened to that race of larger-than-life statesmen.

154. I remember that René Coty, one of France's Presidents during the Fourth Republic, was a member of the Coty perfume family.

155. I remember the first time I ate a doughnut.

156. I remember that, following his suicide, the ashes of Henry de Montherlant were unlawfully sprinkled, from a helicopter, over the Colosseum in Rome.

157. I remember that Graham Greene, uncredited, played a tiny role in Truffaut's *La Nuit américaine*.

158. I remember:

> I know an old woman who swallowed a fly,
> But I don't know why
> She swallowed the fly.
> Perhaps she'll die.

> I know an old woman who swallowed a spider,
> That wriggled and wiggled and *tickled* inside her.
> She swallowed the spider to catch the fly,
> But I don't know why
> She swallowed the fly.
> Perhaps she'll die.

And so it went, through a whole bestiary of creatures, until she swallowed a horse, thereby prompting the rhyming punchline: 'She's dead − *of course*!' But who on earth wrote the song?

159. I remember George Rockwell, leader of the American Nazi Party (and subsequently assassinated?).

160. I remember a *Superman* comic book, one of whose captions read: 'Meanwhile, as Lois Lane was falling off the Empire State Building. . . .'

161. I remember skiffle; and Lonnie Donegan.

162. I remember fretwork.

163. I remember, during the state visit to England of Bulganin and Krushchev, the mysterious disappearance of a

frogman, Commander 'Buster' Crabbe, and wondering whether he could possibly be the same Buster Crabbe who had played Flash Gordon.

164. I remember the question, 'Constantinople is a very big word – how do you spell it?' and the answer, 'i, t.'

165. I remember Hayley Mills in *Pollyanna*; and another Disney film in which she played twin sisters.

166. I remember elephant jokes.

167. I remember the sports commentators Peter Dimmock and Raymond Glendenning.

168. I remember learning the signs for infinity (∞) and pi (π).

169. I remember that, before the advent of ITV, one would hear numerous stories about the comically ill-timed interruption of ads on American television. If these were to be believed, a commercial break invariably eclipsed the winning goal in a football match or the revelation of the murderer's identity in a whodunit.

170. I remember that it was Eric Coates who composed the *Dam Busters* March.

171. I remember Aldermaston marches.

172. I remember Aberfan.

173. I remember a summer craze among children for bizarre little caps from which protruded two antennae.

174. I remember when American students would sell the *New York Herald Tribune* along the Champs-Elysées in Paris (a practice immortalized by Jean Seberg in Godard's *A Bout de souffle*).

175. I remember Ionesco and the Theatre of the Absurd.

176. I remember the defection of Nureyev but, curiously, not that of Baryshnikov.

177. I remember Desperate Dan's cow pies.

178. I remember the extreme pleasure of eating green peas straight from the pod.

179. I remember, from the same period of my life, painting and rolling Easter eggs.

180. I remember the exhibition of a painting with a large hole cut out of its canvas through which a woman's bare breast was inserted.

181. I remember the Ben Barka affair (and I have even stayed in the Paris hotel from which he was abducted).

182. I remember the etymological origin of the acronym 'nylon': 'ny' from 'New York' and 'lon' from 'London'.

183. I remember Pierre Clémenti's gold teeth in Buñuel's *Belle de Jour*.

184. I remember that Anthony Burgess started writing novels after having been advised (incorrectly) by a doctor that he had only a few months to live.

176

185. I remember Mike Sarne.

186. I remember pre-fabs.

187. I remember when Woodbine cigarettes could be purchased in packets of five.

188. I remember, as a child, when shod in Wellington boots, the disagreeable sensation of my socks being dragged down under my heels.

189. I remember Tambimuttu.

190. I remember my embarrassment, when asked by a school chum, 'How does Dvořák go?', because I did not know the answer or even understand the question. (He was referring to the most familiar theme from the 'New World' Symphony.)

191. I remember the film *Davy Crockett* and the adolescent fashion for Davy Crockett hats which it inspired.

192. I remember the Danish musical humorist Victor Borge, each of whose one-man shows seemed a tremendously prestigious affair.

193. The same applied to appearances by the stand-up comedian Mort Sahl.

194. I remember Spiro Agnew declining to visit some blighted urban neighbourhood in an American city with the comment, 'When you've seen one slum, you've seen them all.'

195. I remember marvelling at the massive full-colour comic sections of American Sunday newspapers, which were

forwarded to us by relatives in the United States.

196. I remember Rosemary Brown, whose musical compositions — or so she claimed — had been dictated to her 'from the beyond' by Mozart, Schubert, Chopin, etc.

197. I remember *Telstar*.

198. I remember midi-skirts.

199. I remember crew cuts.

200. I remember that the *New Yorker* published a brief obituary of its office boy.

201. I remember — on live, unscripted television — the journalist Nancy Spain proposing marriage to Gilbert Harding (a personality in whom I took an especial interest, as we shared the same slightly odd and 'effeminate' Christian name).

202. I remember two terrifying TV serials of the fifties: *Epitaph for a Spy*, adapted from a novel by Eric Ambler, and *Little Red Monkey*, of which I remember only the credit titles. These unrolled over the image of a sinister monkey puppet and were accompanied by a theme song ('Little red monkey, funny monkey . . .') which ended in a nerve-jangling shriek. So unsettled was I by that shriek, yet so enthralled by the serial itself, that I would be forced, with each succeeding episode, to invent an excuse whereby I might absent myself from the living-room until the credits were finally off the screen.

203. I remember that the *Billy Cotton Band Show* started with

a huge close-up of Cotton bawling, 'Wakey! Wakey!' and ended with a jolly communal rendering of 'I got a loverly bunch of coconuts'.

204. I remember President Tubman of Liberia.

205. I remember Belinda Lee.

206. I remember road houses.

207. I remember water beds.

208. I remember 'A Wok in the Black Forest'.

209. I remember April Ashley, one of Britain's first transsexuals (or rather, one of the first to refer publicly to her sex-change operation).

210. I remember how disturbed I was by the news photograph of Dr Stephen Ward's body being removed from the flat in Wimpole Mews where, as a consequence of the Profumo scandal, he had committed suicide.

211. I remember, too, the photograph of an anguished young woman crouching over one of the students slain at Kent State University in the sixties; and that, from the same period, of a naked, napalm-scarred child fleeing along a highway in Vietnam.

212. I remember, on television, the credit title sequence of the Harry Worth show: the camera (though, of course, invisible) was positioned, manifestly on the pavement itself, at one end of a street coextensively flanked by a shop window; at the far end of the street, precisely where it formed a right-

angle intersection with another, stood Worth, the right side of his body obscured by the transversal section of the same shop window, with the result that the visible (left) side of his body was 'completed' by its own full-length reflection in that section of the window running parallel to the spectator's viewpoint. When he (Worth) raised his left leg in the air, one therefore had the illusion of both his legs leaving the ground simultaneously (and the prolixity of that description impresses upon me just how difficult it is to convey in words alone the sort of trivial memory which has absolutely no need of them).

213. I remember when, before the Fifth Republic, the British took pleasure in mocking France for the comical rapidity with which each one of its governments would succeed another.

214. I remember the U-2 pilot Gary Powers.

215. I remember that, during Nixon's Presidency, the White House guards were briefly attired in absurd operetta-like uniforms.

216. I remember the joke: 'Apart from that, Mrs Lincoln, how did you enjoy the play?'

217. I remember accompanying my grandmother to a film produced by the Rank Organization. When the studio's logo ('the man with the gong') materialized on the screen, she exclaimed, 'Heavens, I've seen this picture!' — which prompted laughter up to three or four rows away.

218. I remember Uncle Mac's radio request programme on Saturday mornings; and how a request of mine, a song (by

Harry Belafonte? Burl Ives?) which began 'There's a hole in the bucket, dear Liza, dear Liza', was played frequently but never as requested by me.

219. I remember the virtually unchanging routine of the Television Toppers.

220. I remember the Mau-Mau.

221. I remember Paris's 'Golden Boy', François-Marie Banier, a friend and protegé of the ageing poet Aragon and a novelist in his own right, who was photographed for one of the colour supplements decked out in Tadzio's straw hat and sailor-suit from the film of *Death in Venice*.

222. I remember Yves Saint-Laurent's Mondrian mini-skirts, perhaps the ugliest fashion I ever saw.

223. I remember, from the *Archie* comics, Archie himself and his chums Reggie and Jughead.

224. I remember the heatwave of 1976.

225. I remember the kidnapping of Baron Empain.

226. I remember Shirley Abicair and her zither.

227. I remember being puzzled, apropos the American cartoon series *Boss Cat*, by the fact that its theme song referred throughout to the character as 'Top Cat'. I later discovered that it was the existence, in Britain, of a cat food named 'Top Cat' which had forced the BBC to advertise the show under a different title.

228. And, speaking of theme songs, I remember that of *Champion, the Wonder Horse*.

229. I remember once owning an adult-sized bow-and-arrow.

230. I remember that Schopenhauer was the last man known to speak fluent Latin; and that, when the landlady to whom he had owed a large sum of money finally died, he instantly punned, 'Anus obit, onus abit' (meaning 'An old woman dies, a burden is removed').

231. I remember that the 'events' of May '68 in Paris were said to have been precipitated by the expulsion of Henri Langlois from the Cinémathèque Française, of which he was the curator.

232. I remember Gabrielle Russier, a French schoolteacher who fell in love with one of her male pupils, a boy almost thirty years her junior. Whereupon his parents, Marxists both and supposedly liberal in matters of sexual morality, threatened her with confinement in a psychiatric hospital; and the affair ended with her suicide.

233. I remember the 'Invisible Man' unwrapping his bandages.

234. I remember Percy Edwards' animal impersonations.

235. I remember Caryl Chessman.

236. I remember the Christmas Party that used to be the highlight of BBC TV's Christmas Day viewing, and in which various stars of the period (including newsreaders, *Animal,*

Vegetable and Mineral panellists, etc.) would 'let their hair down' by indulging in all kinds of turns, games and charades.

237. I remember Bill and Ben, the Flowerpot Men, and their friend Weed, who would squeal 'We-e-e-ed!' in a falsetto voice. I also remember Andy Pandy, Muffin the Mule and Lenny the Lion (with the ventriloquist Terry Hall).

238. I remember Tommy Manville and his (how many?) wives.

239. I remember, as a child, how I used to scurry out of the sea on to the beach, where I would stand, shivering, my arms trembling at my sides, and wait to be rubbed down with a bath towel.

240. I remember my first pair of long trousers (a rather traumatic social promotion denied today's children, who appear to wear jeans from earliest infancy).

241. I remember a glossy but short-lived magazine named *London Life*.

242. I remember 'I gotta horse!'

243. I remember 'Crawfie'.

244. I remember 'the great imposter' (but, because he assumed so many aliases, I have forgotten his own name).

245. I remember Sylvia Peters and MacDonald Hobley.

246. I remember how, after school, I would accompany my

best friend home on my bicycle before cycling back (across town) to my own house.

247. I remember when there stood, outside cinemas, lollipop-shaped signposts indicating where queues were to form for the variously priced seats: 1/6, 2/3, 3/9, etc.

248. I remember not properly understanding the significance of the expression 'blow job' and believing it to mean that one's sexual organs were breathed over (an idea which, I have to say, I found extremely stimulating).

249. I remember that Lady Barnett committed suicide after having been convicted of shoplifting.

250. I remember *Dotto*.

251. I remember, in the illustrated magazine *Paris-Match*, a spread of excessively graphic photographs of atrocities committed during the Algerian War.

252. I remember that Kenneth Tynan was the first person to use the word 'fuck' on television.

253. I remember 'I tought I taw a puddy cat . . .'

254. I remember streakers.

255. I remember starlets regularly 'losing' their bikini tops at the Cannes Film Festival.

256. I remember — though only just — Sir Horace Cutler, a former leader of the GLC. (Ken Livingstone was a hard act to precede.)

257. I remember watching documentary footage of lemmings leaping *en masse* off a clifftop: from which point, these curious, self-destructive little rodents ceased, for me, to be only a metaphor.

258. I remember the film *Geordie*, in which Bill Travers played a Scottish hammer thrower travelling with the British team to the 1956 Olympic Games in Melbourne. When, at the end, one last hope of victory remains to him, his girlfriend in Scotland breathlessly whispers into the wireless set on which the event is broadcast, 'C'mon, ma wee Geordie!' Whereupon, naturally, he throws his hammer a record-breaking distance.

259. I remember Sophie Tucker, 'the last of the red hot mommas'.

260. I remember a fad for collecting rocks as 'pets'.

261. And I remember the craze for Cabbage Patch Dolls, each of which − or so their manufacturer claimed − was absolutely unique.

262. I remember that, by crossing the index and second finger of my right hand and stroking the bridge of my nose with the X thus formed, I would have the impression of being double-nosed.

263. I remember, as an adolescent, invariably finding myself among the very last to be 'selected' for one or other of two football teams about to play a match in the school playground; and even − the ultimate humiliation − being paired off with another duffer (usually some beaky, bespectacled boy with whom I felt no sense of solidarity) as 'two for the price of one'.

264. I remember buying a copy of the *Evening Standard* because of a news-stand headline that read: FAMOUS FILM STAR DIES. The 'famous film star' turned out to be Jerry Desmonde, familiar to the public only (if at all) as Norman Wisdom's 'straight man'.

265. I remember Michael Fagin, the intruder who breezed into the Queen's bedroom.

266. I remember the publication of Pasternak's *Doctor Zhivago* and Lampedusa's *The Leopard*, perhaps the last European novels (though *The Leopard* is, in fact, a long novella) to have been universally acclaimed as masterpieces; and that of Katharine Anne Porter's *Ship of Fools*, which patently aspired to the same status but was greeted by the majority of critics as shallow, bloated kitsch.

267. I remember the theme music of *Never on Sunday*.

268. I remember the scorpions' square dance from one of Disney's True-Life Adventure films, *The Living Desert*.

269. I remember Ralph Reader and the Gang Shows ('We're riding along on the crest of a wave . . .').

270. I remember the bandleader Joe Loss and his vocalists Dennis Lotis and Lita Roza.

271. I remember Karsh of Ottawa.

272. I remember the very first time I maladroitly sought to adjust the small air-conditioning unit located above one's seat aboard an aeroplane and how mortified I was when a stewardess was required to assist me.

273. I remember the widespread conviction, when the oil

crisis erupted in the early seventies, that it represented a momentous juncture in world history, that we would all have to revert to gas lamps, wood fires, etc.

274. I remember hearing that, in advertisements, wrist-watches are set either at 10.10 or 1.50 so that their dials might 'smile' and therefore appear more desirable to a potential buyer.

275. I remember the navy blue gym slips worn by schoolgirls when playing hockey.

276. I remember Sabrina and the song with which she was associated, 'Climb up the Garden Wall'.

277. I remember winkle pickers.

278. I remember Ron and Eth.

279. I remember Roy Rogers' elaborately stitched cowboy shirts and the bespangled saddles of his horse Trigger.

280. I remember Farouk.

281. I remember 'Float like a butterfly, sting like a bee'.

282. I remember Elmer Rice's *The Adding Machine*, Ugo Betti's *The Queen and the Rebels* and Karel Čapek's *R.U.R.* I remember, too, that the '38' suffix to Jean Giraudoux's *Amphitryon 38* supposedly referred to the number of times the Amphitryon legend had been theatrically adapted.

283. I remember a television panel game, *Why?*, the point of which was that a team of panellists (who included Jimmy

Edwards) would answer, as humorously as possible, a series of whimsical questions, all of them beginning with the word 'Why', posed by the studio audience. (One such question was 'Why are bubbles round?', to which even I, though no expert in scientific matters, was capable of offering an intelligent answer: the roundness of bubbles is caused by the absolute uniformity of the air pressure exerted upon them.) The show was so calamitously received that it was cancelled after only a single broadcast.

284. I remember Patti Hearst and her unfortunate fiancé, Steven Weed.

285. I remember a Japanese student at the Sorbonne, an epigone of Sade and Bataille, murdering a young Dutch girl with whom he was hopelessly in love, then carving up her body and eating it.

286. I remember Alexander Haig being shunted back and forth across the Atlantic during the Falklands crisis.

287. I remember *Amos 'n' Andy*.

288. I remember 'happenings'.

289. I remember 'Duke – Duke – Duke of Earl'.

290. I remember George Lazenby, who played James Bond (for the one and only time) in *On Her Majesty's Secret Service*.

291. I remember that the word 'serendipity' was coined by Horace Walpole.

292. I remember that my very first key-ring was attached to a

tiny red brandy barrel, of a type said to be worn by St Bernard dogs in the Tyrol.

293. I remember Edd 'Kookie' Byrnes.

294. I remember George Painter, the award-winning biographer of Proust, and I have occasionally wondered what has become of him.

295. I remember how much I loathed, in comic books, those stories (usually of historical or Biblical origin) in which, instead of by speech balloons, the narrative was conveyed by discrete blocs of text located above or below the strip of images.

296. . I remember a group of militants for animals' rights claiming to have injected Mars Bars with a poisonous substance − a claim, however, which turned out to be a hoax.

297. I remember the anxiety with which, in my early adolescence, I would follow the erratic progress of my pubic hair; and how one of my school chums, a frizzy-haired boy, was mocked for having 'pubic hair on his head'.

298. I remember Bible class.

299. I remember, from Masefield's poem 'Cargoes', the lines:

Quinquireme of Nineveh from distant Ophir

and

Dirty British coaster with a salt-caked smoke stack

but I have quite forgotten the rest.

300. I remember *Have a Go* with Wilfrid Pickles and, unforgettably, 'Mabel at the table'.

301. I remember my first day at school.

302. I remember Mark Spitz.

303. I remember wondering why Mickey Mouse had, not five, but four fingers.

304. I remember the theme music, 'Sha-ba-da-ba-da', played almost without interruption in the film *Un Homme et une femme*.

305. I remember owning a gyroscope whose support was a miniature Eiffel Tower.

306. I remember *You Are There*, a TV programme in which historical events of note were both dramatized and commentated, as would be, for instance, a state visit or the Opening of Parliament. The most controversial of its subjects was the Crucifixion.

307. I remember the jowly, lugubrious features of Edgar Lustgarten.

308. I remember transfers.

309. I remember *The Perry Como Show*: Como's 'relaxed' sweaters; his bar stool; his song 'Delaware' (whose lyrics punned on a dozen or so American states); and that spot in the show reserved for viewers' requests, a spot introduced by the vocalized refrain, 'Letters — we get letters — we get lots and lots of letters . . .'

310. I remember how, in the initial year of his Presidency, Valéry Giscard d'Estaing would periodically invite himself to dinner at the homes of 'ordinary citizens'; and how, on one much-publicized occasion, he was served *cassoulet*.

311. I remember being especially charmed by my newborn godchild's fingernails.

312. I remember how frustrated I was (and, indeed, still am), when reading certain twentieth-century poets (Eliot, Pound), to encounter quotations in Greek, a language with which I am totally unfamiliar.

313. I remember a film called *Phffft!*

314. I remember Karen Ann Quinlan.

315. I remember rose hip syrup.

316. Which reminds me of Rose Murphy, an Irish singer of sugary ballads.

317. I remember 'discovering' El Greco.

318. I remember being informed that if the rhythm of an eighteenth-century minuet corresponded to that of the phrase 'Are you the O'Reilly who owns this hotel?' then it was one of Haydn's.

319. I remember Tom Lehrer.

320. I remember wet dreams.

321. I remember that insidiously plaguey sensation (which

might continue to nag at one for hours on end) of not being able, *à deux*, to remember either a name or some insignificant factual detail that, separately, would doubtless pose no problem whatsoever. In my own case, the two most protracted instances of this phenomenon concerned the composer of the opera *The Happy Prince* (Malcolm Williamson) and the Italian town in which Max Beerbohm lived as an expatriate (Rapallo – but my interlocutor and I were thrown off course by Ravenna).

322. I remember wondering how often I might fortuitously have figured in the background of snapshots taken by sightseers.

323. I remember Violet Elizabeth Bott lisping, 'I'll thcream, an' thcream, an' thcream till I'm thick' in the *Just William* books.

324. I remember 'Beat the Clock' from *Sunday Night at the London Palladium*.

325. I remember that General de Gaulle retired to the village of Colombey-les-Deux-Eglises.

326. I remember the comedian Reg Dixon and the organist Reginald Dixon.

327. I remember 'Mrs Shufflewick' and 'Mr Pastry' (the latter's real name being Richard Hearne).

328. I remember that Romain Gary, the French novelist, published two novels under the pseudonym of Emile Ajar.

329. I remember 'Che sera, sera, Whatever will be, will be . . .', as sung by Doris Day.

330. I remember my great-grandmother; at least, I think I do.

331. I remember The Temperance Seven.

332. I remember the hairdresser Raymond 'Teazy-Weazy'.

333. I remember that Paul Valéry, Jean-Paul Sartre and Michel Butor published collections of essays under the respective titles of *Variétés*, *Situations* and *Répertoires*.

334. I remember the fashion for immersing one's jeans in a bathtub of water in order to make them shrink.

335. I remember the showman Mike Todd, the wide-screen format that bore his name, Todd-AO, and his production, *Scent of Mystery*, filmed in a process called Smellovision which caused odours to be released into the cinema auditorium at appropriate moments of the plot (a process flippantly nicknamed Todd-BO). Todd was briefly married to Elizabeth Taylor and died in an air crash.

336. I remember Nina and Frederick. Nina (as Nina van Pallandt) has since made a minor career for herself as an actress, but no one appears to know what might have happened to Frederick (a Baron, as I recall).

337. I remember the little black strips perforated by red circles that one inserted into cap pistols.

338. I remember the cowboy star 'Lash' Larue.

339. I remember, too, that the real name of the actor who played Hopalong Cassidy was William Boyd.

340. I remember it being claimed of the singer Alma Cogan that she herself had sewn on all the sequins of her glittery, multi-sequined gowns.

341. I remember how, surrounded by my family, my aunts, uncles and neighbours, I watched the Coronation on a television set which had been acquired a few days before the ceremony; and how, during a tedious stretch of the procession, I endeavoured to 'peer round the corner' of the screen to learn in advance what was coming next.

342. I remember the day Queen Elizabeth was shot at (with a blank) while Trooping the Colour.

343. I remember when it was fairly customary for guardsmen to faint away during a royal inspection (they would seem to be a more robust breed these days).

344. I remember hula hoops.

345. I remember the Monkees.

346. I remember the trial of Lana Turner's daughter Cheryl for the stabbing of her mother's lover, a hoodlum named Johnny Stompanato.

347. I remember never quite knowing, in my relationship with the French, when − or how − to switch from 'vous' to the more familiar 'tu'.

348. I remember two films released in the mid-fifties whose sole points in common were their titles and their absolute nullity: *The Runaway Bus*, starring Frankie Howerd and Margaret Rutherford, and *The Wayward Bus*, starring Jayne Mansfield.

194

349. There also existed two rival film biographies of Oscar Wilde (one with Peter Finch, the other with Robert Morley) and of Jean Harlow (one with Carroll Baker, the other with Carol Lynley).

350. I remember concocting home-made sweets out of sugar, cream, chocolate powder, sultanas, etc. Though on occasion edible enough, these never bore the remotest resemblance to anything one might think of as 'sweets'.

351. I remember a pleasant Sunday afternoon TV programme for children, *All Your Own*, presented by Huw Weldon.

352. I remember 'swapping'.

353. I remember the Frug.

354. I remember the playboy Gunther Sachs.

355. I remember Fyfe Robertson.

356. I remember 'It was an itsy-bitsy teeny-weeny yellow polka-dot bikini . . .'.

357. I remember the day on which, during the Cuban missile crisis, American and Soviet ships were due to confront each other in the Caribbean. It was to happen, if I am not mistaken, at about three o'clock in the afternoon (our time) and, in my school classroom, I remember half-cupping my hands over my ears in anticipation of the inevitable explosion! That strikes me now as, in general, a period when the world would lurch from one such 'crisis' to another — crises which were somehow invested with a far greater urgency than their current equivalents.

358. I remember no less vividly the classical music played, in the immediate wake of President Kennedy's assassination, on both radio and television.

359. I remember the construction of Brasilia.

360. I remember that the première of the film *Underwater*, starring Jane Russell, was held . . . underwater.

361. I remember Steve Reeves in *Hercules Unchained*.

362. I remember when the French Riviera seemed to me impossibly glamorous and inaccessible.

363. I remember sobbing uncontrollably at the death of Jo in *Bleak House* and at that of Lennie in *Of Mice and Men*.

364. I remember attending ABC children's matinees every Saturday morning and singing the club song, which began: 'We are the boys and girls . . .' I remember as well the ABC logo: a crowing rooster perched inside an inverted triangle.

365. I remember the first coffee bars and the thrill of ordering espresso.

366. I remember that, unlike the sort from Brighton and Blackpool, Edinburgh Rock is soft and crumbly.

367. I remember a mass killing at a McDonalds restaurant in the United States.

368. I remember *Gidget*.

369. I remember Pat Boone.

370. I remember that Manfred Mann was the name not of a person but of a pop group.

371. I remember the whole cast disrobing at the end of *Hair*.

372. I remember that, at summer school, sharing a bedroom for the first time in my life, I would demurely sit on that side of my bed which faced away from my room-mate's when removing my underpants.

373. I remember the pleasure I took in watching billboard posters being pasted up and, in particular, noting how the two halves of advertising slogans would be (more or less) effortlessly aligned.

374. I remember when men's glasses invariably lacked a lower rim, and that it was next to impossible to obtain any other design from an optician.

375. I remember Nixonburgers; also 'Billy Beer', marketed by Billy Carter, President Jimmy's rather embarrassing brother.

376. I remember the so-called 'payola' scandal which surrounded the *64,000 Dollar Question* quiz show in the United States.

377. I remember conkers.

378. I remember when one could find LP records of scenes extracted from such films as *Casablanca* and *Gone With The Wind*: the dialogue assigned to their leading actors (in these two instances, Humphrey Bogart and Clark Gable) had been erased from the recording and a script provided so that the

listener could act out his fantasy of a romantic exchange between himself and Ingrid Bergman or Vivien Leigh. The same principle was later applied to a strictly musical context, enabling an amateur pianist to buy a record of the Grieg Concerto, for instance, minus the music specifically composed for the solo instrument.

379. I remember repeatedly hearing, on radio weather forecasts, such terms as 'Ross', 'Cromarty' and 'Force' without ever having the slightest notion as to what they might mean.

380. I remember camps for 'displaced persons' (DPs).

381. I remember *The Flying Enterprise*.

382. I remember Beethoven teeshirts.

383. I remember Princess Grace's fatal car accident and the rumours which circulated concerning precisely who was at the steering-wheel.

384. I remember Sellar and Yeatman, authors of *1066 and All That*.

385. I remember the graffito '. . . rules, OK?'.

386. I remember that the surname of Lucy and Linus in the *Peanuts* strip is van Pelt; and that Andy Capp's next-door neighbours are called Chalkie and Rube.

387. I remember, from reports of Jeremy Thorpe's trial, that one of his business associates was a certain John le Mesurier, who, however, bore no relation to his namesake, a

thin, melancholic character actor (and husband of Hattie Jacques).

388. I remember I used to claim that I could deduce what genre a film belonged to merely by studying the shafts of dust caught in the luminous cone which issued from a projectionist's cabin. (Whatever became of that cone, by the way?)

389. I remember that Mae West never actually said, 'Come up and see me sometime', nor did Garbo ever actually say, 'I want to be alone'.

390. I remember Craven 'A' cigarettes.

391. I remember Action Painting.

392. I remember a mini-quiz presented by the comedian 'Cheerful' Charlie Chester. Its contestants were invited to propose a random sequence of three musical notes, which he would then play on the piano and endeavour to think of a popular tune of which they constituted the opening.

393. I remember watching on television the attempted putsch of a group of Spanish generals.

394. I remember Garry Davis, the 'Citizen of the World', who was constantly arrested at airports and frontiers.

395. I remember Paddy Roberts, a nightclub singer-pianist of songs with slightly risqué lyrics.

396. I remember Terry-Thomas's gap-toothed smile, gaudy waistcoats and elongated cigarette-holders.

397. I remember how neat and pristine the first two or three pages of my school jotters were kept, and how very soon they became dog-eared and ink-stained.

398. I remember 'Katie' advertising Oxo cubes.

399. I remember 'Red' Adair.

400. I remember . . .

(to be continued)

The following pages are at the reader's disposal to add his or her own 'I remembers', if so inclined.